Copyright © 2021 Dick Bell, Seaton, Devon.

Written by Dick Bell MBE
Designed and edited by P. F. Adams

   Scripture quotations [marked NIV] taken from the Holy Bible,
New International Version Anglicised Copyright © 1979, 1984, 2011 Biblica
Used by permission of Hodder & Stoughton Ltd, an Hachette UK Company
All rights Reserved
'NIV' is a registered trademark of Biblica UK trademark number 1448790.
All rights reserved. No part of this publication may be reproduced, stored in
a retrieval system, or transmitted in any form or by any means, electronic,
mechanical or otherwise, without the prior permission in writing from the
copyright owner.

Two Trees Series

First published in 2022 by Dick Bell MBE

God the Scientist.
by Dick Bell MBE

Contents

Prologue: God the Scientist.

Is God scientific? Does He cross all the "T's" and dot all the "I's" that learned scientists know, believe and are constantly discovering? Is God outside the realms of man's learning, or is He an integral participant in learning?

The specialisations of science are multiple. There is research going on today that, like the branches of a tree, are based on yesterday's research, which is based on historical research going back centuries. We research today on top of what other scientists have researched in time past. We are adding new layers of discovery day after day. The average man in the street is benefitting throughout his life from the new discoveries of his scientific contemporaries. We live in an exciting scientific age.

Two things emerge. One is faith, the other is limit.

Take faith first. Today's scientist attempts to develop what his forebears first discovered. He has faith that what his predecessors have written is, indeed, factual truth. Some of it isn't. But he has faith that it is. And, given the development of new instrumentation, he can research what his predecessor(s) couldn't. For example, the advent of DNA in criminology has extended the forensic breadth of evidence, where, only a few decades ago, fingerprints were the best evidence. Before that, blood groups were the best evidence. Before that, circumstances and witnesses formed the best that man could conjure up. So today, all the past systems are still available, but DNA now provides indelible proof of a criminal's guilt. Today's criminologist has faith in the biologist that DNA provides all that the biologist says it does. This principle of faith is incorporated in all scientific research. Without it, no new research could ever take place.

The second is limit. In every area of scientific discipline, there are boundaries beyond which it is impossible to go. Researchers find that, as they forage ahead, some experiments fail completely. That means that their theories become invalid, and honest researchers cease experimenting in that area. For example, in one of the chapters there is a story of research in monkey behaviour, to try to understand if there is a connection between apes and humans in any evolutionary tree. It concerned speech. The researchers, over a period of 3.5 years, 9 hours a day, 7 days a week tried to find if a Bonobo ape could talk like humans. The experiment dismally failed. There was no connection. Evolutionary theory could not be proven in that discipline or along that route. In today's digital revolution, there will be boundaries beyond which man will be unable to go, but *inside* the boundaries, multiple new things will be able to be developed.

Some of the chapters in this book are my own discovery journey. Your journey will differ from mine. But I challenge you to determine whether my journey has been invalid or not. I have discovered that God is involved up to the hilt in every area of science. Indeed, even more than that, that all experimentation in every scientific discipline is enhanced and proven when God is accessed throughout the research. He knows the boundaries, and can steer researchers away from wasting their time and effort, and direct them into discoveries that bless and beautify the rest of earth.

There is no end to scientific development, whatever our interests may be. That is because, in my opinion, there is no end to God. His wisdom, knowledge, creation and care stand alongside all those who want His friendship. We all do much better with Him than without Him.

I pray that you will enjoy my research into science.

God the Scientist.

I have been reading John Lennox' book "God's Undertaker – has Science buried God?" for the third time. How I wish that I was learned enough to be able to absorb and retain all the fascinating information that such a book contains!

Professor John Lennox systematically looks at every aspect of the Theory of Evolution through the eyes and researchers of Geology, Cosmology, Mathematics, Physics, and the whole of the latter half of the book is devoted to Biology. He is a Professor of Mathematics at Oxford University – and a Christian. How lovely it is to have someone of his calibre arguing against the tenets of Darwinian Evolution, taking on those of the same calibre who, often through scientific jargon that few understand, try to persuade us that Evolution is the Real Thing. Biology is the key issue. What is life? How does it differ from inert objects? How did life come about (a thing that no one knows as yet)? What are the probabilities of life occurring spontaneously?

These issues occupy the minds of many researchers around the globe, all moving in that general direction through the avenues of their specific specialities. John Lennox is very careful to quote experts in all the fields and his conclusions are, as Melanie Phillips of the Spectator writes, "An excoriating (i.e. attacking) demolition of Dawkins' overreach from biology into religion." In my words, he makes mincemeat of Evolution as a valid world view of the origins of this cosmos.

He is careful to point out the difference between "micro" and "macro" evolution, micro being readily observed and observable, but macro being absent from any global observations or even statistics. So, development and variety within a Kind (a biblical word) is very clear and undisputed. Evolution *between* species or kinds, such that a cow could be related in any way to a horse or a pig or any other living creature simply does not exist – in any of the scientific disciplines. It would be pointless for me to quote much from the book; you are best reading it yourself if you are interested.

But let me give you a few quotes to whet your appetite.

"It is argued that an alteration in the ratio of the expansion and contraction forces by as little as 1 part in 10^{55} at the Planck time (just 10^{-43} seconds after the origin of the universe), would have led to either too rapid an expansion of the universe with no galaxies forming or too slow an expansion with consequent rapid collapse" (Page 71).

Eminent mathematician Sir Roger Penrose's calculations "led him to the remarkable conclusion that the 'Creator's aim' must have been accurate to 1 part in 10^{123}, that is 10 followed by 123 zeros, a 'number which it would be impossible to write out in the usual decimal way, because even if you were to put a zero on every particle in the universe there would not even be enough particles to do the job'".

Astrophysicist Hugh Ross lists many such parameters that have to be fine-tuned for life to be possible, and makes a rough but conservative calculation that the chance of one such planet existing in the universe is about 1 in 10^{30} (Page 72).

"Among the many different kinds of amino acids there are twenty involved in making proteins, so if we had a pool consisting of all twenty the probability of getting the correct amino acid at a specific site in the protein would be 1/20. Thus the probability of getting 100 amino acids in the correct order would be $(1/20)^{100}$, which is about 1 in 10^{130}, and therefore vanishingly small…"

"Yet life as we know it requires hundreds of thousands of proteins, and it has been calculated that the odds of producing these by chance is more than $10^{40,000}$ to 1." (Page 129).

"Gödel believes that mechanism in Biology is a prejudice of our time which will be disproved. In this case, one disapproval, in Gödel's opinion, will consist in a mathematical theorem to the effect that the formation in geological times of a human body by the laws of physics (or any other laws of a similar nature), starting from a random distribution of the elementary particles and the field, is as unlikely as the separation by chance of the atmosphere into its components." (Page 161).

The DNA, which microbiologists have been discovering and unravelling over the last 50 or so years, is laden with information. The human cell is itself laden with countless little protein motors which process this information in such a manner as to form a human being in 9 months. The unique DNA in one sperm (and they are all unique in their trillions) and the unique DNA in one egg blend to form a further unique combination that is you and me. That determines our gender, our size, our colour, our intellectual abilities, our artisan abilities, our fingerprints, our arms and legs, our electrical nervous system, our digestive system, all our internal organs, and, to cap it all, our character and personality. Because the conceiving is human, we end our time in the womb as fully human, with a soul, a spirit and a body that is, for the most part, beautiful and fully formed. Parents with very little scientific knowledge – and even those with much – are astonished that half an hour's sexual fun can end up with a fully formed human being. It's miraculous.

Even scientists whose hard-headed task in life is to unearth the inner workings of the cell ought to be astonished at its complexity, its intricacy, its accuracy and its exquisite nature. Many are.

John Lennox points out that knowing the information contained in the DNA (the genome) still does not produce life. Even when we have learned all the codes derived from the DNA information (which we have not yet achieved), it still does not indicate how that cell and those cells are *living*. Our natural experience is that the human soul brings life to the human body, and when the soul departs the body dies. It no longer has life. But what about animals, insects and all living creatures? What happens when they die? So what is a soul?

My search for who God is continues. Reading books like that of John Lennox' simply opens up more avenues of wonder and astonishment at God's nature. So what is He?

He is a perfect scientist.

God didn't just "make" animals. He designed them, constructed them, manufactured them carefully, thoughtfully, exquisitely. DNA, and all its associated complexity, is as ancient as life itself, although we have only unearthed it, named it and discovered it during my lifetime. No animals or humans could have existed without their complex DNA from the beginning. And when was the beginning? And how did living things suddenly appear, along with all their complexity and variety?

The astonishing thing is that they all work. Everything works. Gravity works. The atmosphere still sits on top of the earth and does not dissipate into space. The magnetic core still works, providing a security blanket over the earth. Trees and plants still get sown and reaped. Animals get born, live and die, but do not diminish in number. The whole of earth's systems still go on working. The cosmos is fine-tuned so accurately that earth (the only one we know for certain in existence) supports life and us. We had no hand in our birth. None of us chose to be born. (Jesus, the only human to pre-exist His birth, was the only human who chose to be born). The fact that we are alive and can read this chapter is a living miracle; we have no right to be alive at all. There is no reason why we should exist, and, as I said, it involved no choice of our own. If earth really is the only planet in existence in the universe (and there is every reason to believe it is and no actual evidence to the contrary), then why are we? What is the purpose of our being here?

The answer to that surely cannot be just to "do stuff" on earth, can it? Our life span of 70 odd years is far too short a time to make any difference to this earth. No human being, in all the millennia of their existence, has altered the earth and its ability to support life. Politicians can influence the running of the earth while they are in office, but they soon go. Ronald Regan and Maggie Thatcher both got Alzheimer's and followed (or will follow) Khrushchev into the next world. They were all very influential in their day. But they have gone. As I will. And you will. So why are you here?

If God is the God He says He is, and if He put this universe together, He must be the Scientist of all scientists. God does not do science. He did not use chemistry and physics to make living creatures. He *is* chemistry and physics. That is part of His nature. In forming the earth and its living creatures, God did it His way. The fact that human chemists and physicists can now discover how it all works simply means that they are uncovering the nature of the Manufacturer. He is the God of the infinitely small, of the intricate detail, of the mathematically perfect. Every cell is vital in His constructions, as is every atom.

In addition, He has given *man* the ability to discover who He is by what He did. What chemists and biologists are unearthing today is astonishing to us outsiders, and wonderful in the extreme. So God has given mankind the ability to discover. Einstein said, "The incomprehensible thing about the universe is that it is comprehensible." Certainly, no one else we know can comprehend or discover it. Monkeys can't. Aliens from outer space can't (because there aren't any). Only man. Only you and me.

We can discover these things because God is allowing us to meet Him and get to know Him. Understanding our own limited discipline of science is one of the avenues He has opened for us to find out how astonishing and astounding He surely is.

But we don't have to be a scientist and read science to get to know God. Lesser mortals can get to know Him in their own way. For the majority of people (that is, the non-scientists) getting to know God involves the simple exercise of personal surrender to His Sovereign Royalty – regardless of any skill set we may or may not have.

So, in that context, consider Jesus. According to our Bibles, Jesus was God from the beginning, and it was He who "manufactured" the cosmos (Col 1:15-20). But the man Jesus recorded in our Bibles was not a scientist at all, so how could He have done all that? The Bible's answer is that He shed His divinity and all that that implies, and became, as a man, humbler and more self-effacing than any other human being has ever been. He lived all His 33 years on earth completely subservient to God, only saying and doing what His Father told Him to say and do. And that, He said, was the best and only way to please God and to live a human life. All our skills must be devoted to God and placed under His direction, and not devoted to our own ends or anyone else's. So, we can have the privilege of being a scientist and getting to know the wonder and excellence of this magnificent creation in which we live, or being a simple, penniless individual with few talents and fewer ideas, yet still be part of the Manufacturer's dance and song in His universe. His promise is that we shall reign with Him for ever after we leave this earth. Just as Jesus has now taken on again all the magnificence of full Divinity from the limited human He was on earth, so we are promised that our future with Him will be infinitely more superior than our present limited earthen humanity. We are going to be perfect, fully able, fully equipped, fully beautiful, and fully sinless and faultless in heaven. That's what Jesus has promised to make us - but only those who love and serve Him here on this temporary earth.

Wouldn't it be nice to create new and unique living creatures, exactly as He has created our present bodies, knowing exactly what we are doing with atoms and amino acids and proteins and DNAs? But creating creatures that last for ever in God's new universe; not like ones that die in ours.

When you dream, dream big. When you worship, worship big. When you do science, do it His way.

God's Laws.

Everyone designs new things after the nature of their character. Artists, musicians and sculptors are good examples. No two artists would paint one scene the same. The uniqueness of their characters drives their pictures in a direction that satisfies their soul's pleasure, style and uniqueness perfectly. Artists *like* the pictures they paint, even though other people may or may not. Even when commissioned to paint for another, the picture reflects the artist's character, not the character of the person or scene being painted, nor the one who commissioned them. The paintings of royalty and noblemen of old are unlikely to be exactly as they might have wished, but are as the artists *thought* they ought to look like.

As I walk round the markets in Nicaragua, I marvel at the huge variety of pottery, necklaces, bracelets and earrings that are on display. Using the same materials, the artisans create very different pieces. Indeed, I have difficulty selecting a present for my daughter from them, because I am not certain what she might like out of all the choice that I am presented with.

Because every person is unique, there is no end to the amazing variety of artistry that will present itself to the onlooker. Every piece is an external reflection of the internal nature of the artist. And because there are so many people in the world there will never be an end to the unlimited variety of work that comes out of them. Even politicians do their politics differently, but all according to the characters they have been born with. So whatever our gifts or talents may be, they emerge from us in a style that cannot be copied or repeated. They can be admired or followed, but never duplicated. Variety is the spice of life, someone said. Indeed it is. And variety is the perfect reflection of the Designer of this universe.

Let me follow that thought and go deeper. On this earth there is an unquantifiable variety of vegetation – trees, bushes, flowers, grasses – all different from each other. There are 26,000 species of Orchid, plus 100,000 hybrids, and 22,000 species of daisy. The same variety is true of animals, insects, fish and birds. But that is not all. Each bird, tree, fish, insect or animal in its kind or species differs from every other one of the same kind or species. No two Pekinese dogs are alike. Nor two Guernsey cows. There is no replication in any species of any kind of anything living. Nor, for that matter, of anything dead. There are no two mountain ranges alike, or lakes, or nations. One author I read talked about the *wastefulness* of creation. It is super-abundant, extravagant, unnecessarily over-provided. It is carelessly, endlessly, beautifully lavish. That also applies to all the opportunities we have in life.

The only things that are replicated here on earth are things that man makes. But even they differ in detail. No two Nissan Micra cars are exactly the same, although the manufacturers try to make them so. But in nature, nothing is the same.

So what *is* the same? The laws that hang all things together are the same. They do not change.

This universe – or at least the observable earth – continues to function according to inviolable and eternal laws that have never changed. Once discovered or realised, they provide an absolute certainty that governs any activity that we may be doing. They are utterly consistent and utterly reliable. They are all mathematically perfect. That, by definition, is what a law in nature is. And they have been in existence from the beginning of earth.

It has taken man many centuries to unravel these laws. Mathematics governs the physics and chemistry laws, and it has taken mathematical geniuses like Newton and Einstein to quantify them for us. Quantifying these laws has not changed the laws. Nor has it invented them. The fact that we now know *how* a bird flies has never affected bird flight. All it has enabled us to do is to copy the birds and make aeroplanes. Understanding the laws that have been on earth from the beginning only enables us to use those same laws in other creative ways. No human *invents* new mathematical laws. He only discovers them. Then by experiment, confirms them.

So, in this observable earth, we see unchanging natural laws round which the whole creation hangs together consistently and reliably, and from which an enormous variety spring. The reproduction of this huge variety of species is infinitely variable, such that no two living things are the same as any other. No two blades of grass are the same.

Nor any two human beings. We now know enough about the human genome to know that in each DNA the number of permutations at the amino acid level is $20^{1,000,000}$ or approximately $10^{1,300,000}$. That is 1 with one million, three hundred thousand noughts after it. Since each DNA is different, the combinations of one sperm and one egg that make human beings, each with a different DNA, are infinite.

So let us extrapolate backwards. The Bible says that God made man in His own image. So who we are and what we are is a reflection of the God who made us. As is the creation in which we walk. If that is so, then we have a God of infinite capacity and infinite beauty, and who is a mathematical genius. If we were to continue to be logical, then we would assume that every living and dead thing, right down to the minutest particle, is governed by unchanging laws that hold everything together in one huge, consistent, harmonised whole. Clearly, we have not yet evaluated every law of the universe. But it is safe to say that they are there, and waiting to be discovered.

This is *God's* creation. That is His personal claim. Not ours. He made it. He holds it together after His style. His is the right to bring it to any conclusion He wants to. But the one thing we can rely on is His consistency. He cannot deny Himself.

In the same way that each artist produces their creations consistently after the uniqueness of their individual characters, so God has reproduced earth and the cosmos after the consistency and fullness of His character.

We cannot escape either Him or His laws. We are integral with this creation and part of God's cosmos – whether we like it or not. There is no other life or existence outside this creation to which we can escape. So, being trapped inside God's creation, it would be logical and sensible to surrender to this creation and its laws. Surrendering to the laws of the universe enables individuals to flourish and grow; rebelling against them is guaranteed to bring disaster and death. Thus, if you stop eating or drinking, you die. Or if you jump off a cliff, you either hurt yourself badly or die. Guaranteed.

So it would therefore be logical and sensible to discover the nature of the Creator of this universe. If we cannot escape Him, it is sensible to follow Him. The more people follow His laws the greater their own creativity and internal peace. Everything works if you work within the laws. The more people rebel against His laws, the more they invite disaster. No one can successfully swim against the flow of the universe.

It must be obvious to everyone that if you follow the manufacturer's instructions you get the best out of your machine. It is also inevitable that to disregard or to rebel against eternal laws is going to land us in trouble. Nothing will succeed that way. But by our choice we are permitted to mutiny, and to be shown that that way ends in failure. It always will. It's inevitable. I quote C. H. Spurgeon: "No one can sin successfully."

What we do happens. That is also as certain as day following night. Selwyn Hughes said: "Obey and get results; disobey and get consequences."

It must also be obvious that mathematical laws are not the only ones we need to adhere to. There are moral laws too, which are just as important and just as sacrosanct. God is a moral as well as a mathematical God. If, inside, you harbour hatred, resentment, bitterness or revenge, you cannot live a life of inner peace because those kinds of things contravene God's nature, and therefore the whole of Nature. God is a God of love, peace, reconciliation, promotion, forgiveness and grace. So He says. So, rebelling against that aspect of His nature invariably brings disaster. Following those aspects of His nature brings us into great peace with both the universe and with everyone else. Loving and affirming people, like God does, makes everyone of us happy people – both the giver and the receiver.

The point I want to make is that if we line ourselves up with all the laws of the universe (God's laws), both moral and scientific, everything we do is guaranteed success. Our creativity and peace will both be immense.

But my Bible says that it is more than that.

God says that He wants a close, personal and intimate relationship with each one of us. That is just another law. What is more, He has made that possible and very available to every single human being on earth. He tells us He is a *personal* God.

Indeed, that is God's carefully prepared way of enabling any human being to know His laws, to obey them and to achieve success. No one but God knows all the laws of the universe. But if we get to know the God who designed and made them, and simply obey Him, then we automatically line up with every universal law. God knows them all, so He will never ask us to do anything that contradicts His knowledge or His nature. That applies to both moral as well as scientific laws.

Every time we obey God and do what He asks of us, the whole of the universe lines up behind us. Every law in the cosmos springs into action and *guarantees* that the thing we are doing happens. Moreover, it will be a thing of excellence, goodness, kindness, and beauty. Because that is God's nature, the things He does through us take on the beautiful nature of the creator of the universe. Because everything God has made is a reflection of His nature, everything

He continues to do through you and me continues to reflect that beautiful and good nature. It cannot be otherwise. Like each one of us, what God does reflects His character perfectly.

That will include healing. Disease is not part of God's nature. Therefore when He asks us (or lets us) pray for a person to be healed from a disease, it works.

It also includes stopping storms raging – as Jesus did on Galilee. Or stopping and starting the rain coming – as Elijah did before wicked King Ahab. Or even stopping the sun going down – as Joshua did when conquering Canaan. Or gaining victory over giants – as Caleb did when he was 85 years old.

That thought brought up the Bible to me. There are certain spiritual rules that God really does want us to know, so He has carefully prompted the Biblical writers to write them so that we can read them. Now this you can absolutely guarantee – that if we adhere to those rules which God has got written down in His Bible, our whole lives will work and be very successful. Obedience is written there. So is *"A man reaps what he sows."* (Gal 6:7). So is *"Live by the Spirit, and you will not gratify the desires of the sinful nature."* (Gal 5:16). So is *"Let the peace of Christ rule in your hearts."* (Col 3:15).

So what about some other spiritual laws?

- Every prayer that we pray that has begun in the heart of God has the answer YES.

- Every word we speak that was first given to us by the Holy Spirit and used when He prompts us sows eternal seed in the heart of the listener. It *will*. It will teach the listener something new he never thought of before. It will direct or correct him according to what he needs then. It will remain in his heart for ever – because it is an eternal word and not a human word. Even if his human mind forgets it, the Holy Spirit will remind him of it in time to come for whenever it is needed next. John 14 and the latter half of 1 Corinthians 2 tells us all that.

- If a man is listening to God as he reads his Bible, he will invariably be spoken to by the Holy Spirit and will learn new things from God. Always. *The Holy Spirit* is the only Teacher of eternal truth, and He will teach anyone who really wants to know what God's heart, character, will and lifestyle are.

- As a man worships God, he opens himself up to discovering the will of God and unravelling the character of God. *"A time is coming and has now come when the true worshippers with worship the Father in spirit and in truth, for they are the kind of worshippers the Father seeks."* (John 4:23).

- Here's another eternal law: *"Remain in me and I will remain in you. No branch can bear fruit by itself; it must remain in the vine. Neither can you bear fruit unless you remain in me."* (John 15:4).

- *"If a man remains in me and I in him, he will bear much fruit; apart from me you can do nothing."* (John 15:5). That is a further eternal and unchanging law of the universe, and is the only way a human being can "bear much fruit". That is, for his life to be eternally and bountifully successful.

So, "All you powers in the heavens above, BOW DOWN. All you powers in the earth below, BOW DOWN, and acknowledge that Jesus Christ is Lord." None of those powers can succeed against the basic laws of the Universe, much less against their Creator. But I can succeed against every one of those other powers, heavenly and earthly, by aligning myself with God's laws and loving their Creator.

Wherever we find things on earth that do not conform to God's good laws (whether scientific, moral or political), we can stop them, rearrange them, adjust them or correct them, and we can know that the whole of the universe – all the laws of nature and all of God's power and purposes – will line up behind us and make our corrections happen.

Let me explain what it has done within me. Suddenly I knew that if I lined myself up fully with God's moral and spiritual laws, then everything I did would be successful. It would work. So this week I had to go to a Primary School to talk about Nicaragua. I knew that the appointment was from God, and that what I had prepared was also from Him. Therefore, I now reasoned, what I did (in my own peculiar style) would prosper enormously, and that God would be there and teach the children all sorts of things that I could not. It was a confidence thing. Instead of going there and hoping that God would bless (but not really being certain), and going out in faith that something may (or may not) occur, I went out in full confidence that the things I put in about the Lord would germinate inside many of the children, bring them into the certainty of God's love in their lives, and start to change them inside. It was *guaranteed*. Lining up with God's will and God's spiritual laws would bring and actually brought spiritual results. Even the teachers were thrilled and were changed as a result of my visit. *"As the rain and the snow come down from heaven and do not return to it without watering the earth and making it bud and flourish, so that it yields seed for the sower and bread for the eater, so is my word that goes out from my mouth: it will not return to me empty, but will accomplish what I desire and achieve the purpose for which I sent it."* (Isaiah 55:10-11). That is, it WILL achieve the purpose for which God sent it. It's inevitable. It's as certain as night following day. Or that which goes up eventually must come back down. Notice the physical laws and the spiritual laws combining in that scripture.

How do we come to this position of absolute confidence?

The Bible makes it very simple. It says: *"Without faith it is impossible to please God, because anyone who comes to him must believe that he exists and that he rewards those who earnestly seek him."* (Heb 11:6). There are rungs of faith, which can only be surmounted by being gifted by the Holy Spirit. Below it, we struggle with faith (will it work or won't it work?). Above it we live over the circumstances, dismiss all negatives, leap over all hindrances, pray with purpose and power, and accomplish things that others would describe as impossible.

After all, if the whole universe is lined up behind us and is thrusting us forward, how can what we do be anything other than successful?

"I pray that out of his glorious riches he may strengthen you with power through his Spirit in your inner being, so that Christ may dwell in your hearts through faith. And I pray that you, being rooted and established in love, may have power, together with all the saints, to grasp how wide and long and high and deep is the love of Christ, and to know his love that surpasses knowledge—that you may be filled to the measure of all the fullness of God. Now to him who is able to do immeasurably more than all we ask or imagine, according to his power that is at work within us, to him be glory in the church and in Christ Jesus throughout all generations, for ever and ever! Amen." (Eph 3:16-21).

Evolution.

I define "A World View" as the basic philosophy – the mind set - that governs an individual's life and actions. It's the reason why we think what we think and it frameworks how we think. That personal world view then determines what we do and why we do it. Why do some people want to make money? Why do terrorists terrorise? Certainly, every educated adult has a world view, and I suspect that every uneducated one does too. How can any human adult do anything unless they first have a reason and purpose for doing it? That reason and purpose is their personal world view, and often changes with time and circumstances.

Because we live in a global village where slick communication at the speed of light instantaneously informs us of every disaster that happens in every corner of the world, global philosophies tend to dominate the earth one at a time as well. Good communication informs us of many other things than disasters.

My (our) life has entertained many global philosophies (that is, world views) that have dominated the world. I was born into the era of Imperialism – where I was a child of the British Raj in Kenya. Fascism led to the Second World War. The winning of that war opened the door to Communism. Then Democracy countered Communism. All these are global world views. When I joined the RAF, I had to do some serious thinking about it. Why did I want to serve the UK's world view (democracy) and fight for it? Why did I reject the communist world view and fight against it? In the end, the major thing that persuaded me that communism was wrong was its deliberate twisting of definitions of words - a rearrangement of truth. Where in my life Right and Wrong were absolutes and all the world conformed to those absolutes, communism redefined words to relate to Communist philosophies not absolutes. It was that lack of integrity and deliberate twisting of recognised universal truth that showed me just how wrong it was, and why I should fight against it. But please don't get me wrong. Certainly, I am an activist and not a pacifist. But I really wanted to have fun flying nice and challenging aeroplanes and tear a few more holes in the sky, and the threat of war and death was one of those mini side-effects that I felt I had to endure for the sake of achieving my goal. My world view at that time was to have fun.

Then I became a Christian.

A living encounter and consequent relationship with Jesus Christ kicked in absolutes absolutely. Now I became as polarised as Communists. The revelation that Jesus was alive, was living and active and was available to know personally cleared every jungle in my head. Now I could see clearly. Now I knew what the whole purpose of earth and creation had been established for, and, above all, that Jesus Christ was Sovereign Lord God Almighty and everything in heaven and on earth was related to him as Lord. Every other philosophy on earth now had a benchmark, a world view by which all other world views could be measured, assessed and judged. Regardless of its intellectual rationale, of the source from which it came, every world view was to be set alongside Christianity and compared with it to see if it had permanence (God alone being the only permanence in the universe). Even democracy. Jesus is the best. But if you don't have Him, democracy is acceptable. John Stott gave me clarity over this in his excellent book "Issues Facing Christians Today". At least democracy has a base philosophy of peace. Democracies choose a government in a peaceful way. And democratic governments generally seek global peace rather than war. Democracy aggressively *protects* its peaceful philosophy, rather than aggressively *spreading* its philosophy by war. Well, normally.

But it is not quite enough to hold firmly to Christianity. To do so blindly without at least considering why other philosophies do not compare with it is to be lopsided. Like young Muslims today, totally sold on Islam, who have never considered any other world view. I was then as lopsided and probably as emotional as they are now (the intense idealism of youth). Consequently, I not only need to know why I like Christianity, I need to know why I don't like others - Fascism, Communism, Humanism, Atheism, New Age or Islam. Or Evolution.

So why don't I like Evolution? Christianity is obviously my main reason, of course. Evolution is deliberately atheistic, is man centred, and has far too many examples of straight deception in it over the last century of its existence so I thought that, having written a few books now which are very pro-Christianity, I would unravel some of the reasons why I think (*I* think) Evolution is a non-starter.

The simple truth is that, concerning the origin of the Universe, no one has any *absolute* proof whatsoever. Neither for Creation (God wants us to walk by faith in Him and His revelation of origins in Genesis rather than discovered evidence (although Romans 1:20 suggests that the observable design evidence of creation points to the Creator and man is without excuse!)), nor for Evolution (no one but God was there at the time). We either have to walk by faith in God or faith in science and scientists. Take your choice. But there is no alternative – it is *faith* or nothing. What I do know is that God is consistent and has neither changed His mind nor His record in Genesis for 3500 years, but scientists are always changing theirs. Most scientists (at least the honest ones) acknowledge that they still do not have all the answers. There are many anomalies they have no solutions to, but their faith is strong enough to assure us all that, bit by bit, the scientific solutions will emerge to justify their evolutionary beliefs.

Just in case you had not realised it, Evolutionary science is now a faith religion. They have taunted Christians in time past that Christianity is believing in something for which there is no evidence and no rationale - so why should anyone believe it? But we can now face them with the same accusation – Molecule to Man Evolution (goo-to-you-via-the-zoo) is a theory for which there is no empirical evidence and which they believe regardless of any empirical evidence that is clearly contrary to that philosophy. Moreover, it has all the other trappings of a religion. Scientists are its high priests. Selected ones are evangelists (like Richard Dawkins). Their rationale is laced with controversy. And, like religious fundamentalists the world over, when in difficulty they respond "Science says ..." Just like others who say "The Bible says ..." or "The Qur'an says ..." - as if science is a closed shop confined to specific intellectuals and information about its secrets is hidden in a few geniuses. "The Guru says, so it must be true" and they assume, probably correctly, that none of the rest of us knows what on earth they're talking about, and can con us that their "beliefs" are facts, hiding them inside scientific jargon that only very few limited experts are familiar with. How different is the God of the Bible - full of integrity, honesty, light and truth. And, hopefully, as all Christians are too.

That's enough background. I have already written in my first book about my own journey from Evolution to Faith in Genesis. So now let me give you the reasons why I think Evolutionary theory does not hold water. I fully accept that my reasons will neither please all nor satisfy all. But I trust that, if you are a person of intellectual integrity, you will look carefully at these evidences I present and at least consider them.

Origins.

The Big Bang theory is the currently accepted scientific model of the origin of the universe where Nothing exploded. A primeval atom of microscopic size with an unmentionably huge density containing all the matter in the cosmos, suddenly appeared from Nothing and Nowhere, and then exploded. No one can give a reason why that Nothing exploded. No one knows where it came from. In science there has never been an explosion that brought order - indeed, the whole rationale for an explosion is to bring *dis*order. Yet the scientists believe and say that this one explosion brought about the beautiful order seen throughout the Universe. Strange. They have no other rationale for the origin of matter, or of energy. There are four things no science can provide an answer to: the origin of matter, the origin of energy, the origin of mathematics, and the origin of life.

The size of the universe is so vast and the observable matter within it so sparse that scientists have invented matter they cannot observe to make the Big Bang theory work. The only way they can account for the forces holding the galaxies together is to have matter counterbalancing the observable matter. This unseen matter, (in fact nine times the visible matter), they called dark matter, exotic particles in black space, black holes and all sorts of other inventions. This dark matter has never been seen or attested, and has no scientific or observable evidence; it is still only theory. Scientific Christians who believe in Intelligent Design and Creation find the invention of so much dark matter wholly unconvincing, and note the theory is driving the invention of observations. Truthfully, at present there remains a great deal of mystery about the universe. But Christians know a Designer who understands it all and has a handle on all the problems it presently gives us!

Biology, Anthropology, Geology and Cosmology.

The three disciplines of Biology (and its associate Anthropology), Geology and Cosmology need billions of years to justify their science. Biology is the main one, because you need billions of years of life to believe that every creature on earth, from fish, birds, insects, animals to man are all inter-related, and have all descended in one family tree from one life-giving one-celled organism. Biology was the specialisation of Charles Darwin who gave this atheistic religion its major boost. Geology is the second and is linked with Biology. To get billions of years for the evolution of life you need billions of years of Geology. The third is Cosmology. Stars that are billions of light-years away needed billions of years before their light is observable on earth. Hence the world view of these three disciplines tends to be that of Evolution - Evolution needs those billions of years for their disciplines to be considered reasonable and respectable. It is interesting that there are many scientists in other disciplines - Mathematics, Physics, Chemistry, medicine and others who are either creationists or believe in Intelligent Design (ID). Those who do not *need* billions of years are more likely to be happy with only the few thousand of the Bible. Hence the disparity among scientists - and the debates.

So what in Biology do I think doesn't tie up with the billions of years of Evolution?

Time.

___

When I was a boy at school, Evolution needed 3 billion years for its family tree to reproduce from the original one-celled amoeba. Now that time frame has extended to 15 billion years, and 4.6 billion years for the age of the earth. But there is a mathematical difficulty involved in this, and I thank Andrew Sibley for pointing this out to me and presenting us with facts. (I evaluate this quote in the next paragraph). I quote verbatim from his book "The timeframe of 10^{18} seconds for the age of the universe can be multiplied by the possible number of molecules in the observable universe (10^{80}) if it were full of organic soup of amino acids, and multiplied by the highest frequencies of gamma rays (10^{20} per second) to give the total number of possible events in the universe (10^{118}). This number can then be compared with the number of permutations in human DNA at the amino acid level ($20^{1,000,000,000}$ or approximately $10^{1,300,000,000}$). In fact just one essential protein such as hexosaminidase A contains 529 amino acids with 20^{529} permutations (or 10^{688}). The mismatch between the level of complexity in DNA and possible events in the universe is staggering."[1]

This calculation for the number of possible events in the universe is known as the Universal Probability Bound and determines the upper limit in which time and chance can work in the universe. There are slightly different ways of formulating it, and William Dembksi[2] has popularised it well, but the end result is the same, that even with unrealistic assumptions time and chance fail by an unimaginably huge margin even to begin to construct functional organic molecules. 10^{18} seconds is 15 billion years. The universe is not full of organic soup, neither is it crammed full of gamma rays, thankfully. In fact gamma rays destroy the genetic code through the production of mutations and amino acid links via peptide bonds at a rate of about 50 per second not 10^{20} per second. Gamma rays would fry everything in sight! In human DNA there are *four* types of nucleotides, A T C and G and 20 types of amino acid. There is no possibility of there being sufficient time and space in the universe to effect the biological changes claimed by Evolution.

Leaving aside the mathematical argument for a moment, it's fascinating to see that these four nucleotides, A, T, C and G in the DNA form the code for all living things. Each sperm has its own unique set of codes, as does each egg. Together they form a unique combination from which we all come. These codes programme the proteins so that they gather together to form all the functions inside the body that process through the formation and maintenance of the body. They even decide on the form and shape of our body, our gender and what we look like. DNA is, perhaps, the most complex helix known in the universe. Each one is different. Without that preset and infinitely variable information, no body would form or have life.

So where did that very precise and intelligent coding come from? Human, animal and vegetable life *start* with a highly complex and very intelligent design code.

Mutation.

Today Darwin's thesis stands or falls on mutations. The theory is that mutations caused by some random process such as chemical poisoning or radiation alters DNA in a creature, and this allegedly leads to improvement in the species. There are no other theories accounting for changes in DNA. Now I have discovered some interesting stuff about mutations.

First of all, practically *all* mutations are detrimental. Mutations work on the DNA. They do not enhance the original animal; they detract from it. "Most mutations are deleterious, slightly deleterious or in the best case neutral." (Hans Degens, Origins 45 Feb 2007, P13). Mutations lose legs, alter eyes and misshape bodies. All mutations take a creature downhill not uphill. Evolutionists claim that birds have evolved from reptiles such as dinosaurs. But the gap between the structure of reptiles and birds is so vast in terms of the number of alterations that it takes a lot of faith to believe it could ever happen. The gaps are immense and include a totally different lung system involving unidirectional airflow through five air sacs, a rearward sloping pelvic bone structure that expands the air sacs via attachment to the spinal column, *and* lack of the diaphragm, not to mention the problem of evolving flight feathers, leave alone the change from reptile to mammal. Any intermediate form could not survive long enough to pass on its genes. Faith is needed because there is no evidence for any of it. Scientists are desperate to find "Missing Links". But there are thousands of missing links that would be required to change a reptile to a bird, and there is no evidence of any anywhere. Besides, how could a deteriorated mutation reproduce effectively? Reproduction is always unpredictable. Don't two intelligent humans sometimes produce mentally handicapped children? And don't two mentally handicapped parents sometimes produce intelligent offspring? Both at times certainly. And shouldn't there have to be two identical mutations to produce a third in the chain towards permanent change? There are enormous problems and paradoxes in fixing so many mutations in whole populations. So far as I can read, no one has been able to observe or reproduce the progeny of *one* mutation that was predictable, consistent and an improvement on its parents.

At the turn of the 20th century, Pearl Raymond (a distinguished American Biologist) experimented on the fruit fly *Drosophila,* followed by Thomas Hunt Morgan in 1910. It had the advantage of having a very short life span of two weeks, and experiments could follow fast and easily. They bombarded the flies with ultraviolet radiation, altering their DNA. They certainly got mutations. Offspring with different shaped bodies, different numbers of legs, wings out of their heads etc appeared. Mating the mutations with others and bombarding them with ultraviolet radiation produced weirder offspring. The DNA allowed for anomalies to occur, but it was boundaried. "Raymond failed, after breeding *Drosophila* to three hundred generations, over fifteen years, to alter the genes."[3] He could go so far, and no further. It is the same in insects, birds, fish, animals and vegetation. Man has very successfully been able to change animals and vegetables by selective breeding, and we call this Adaptation, but it turns out that the information for such diversity is in the genetic code in the first place by design. People have differently coloured eyes, hair and skin, which makes for a more colourful world, but we are all human beings. But Adaptation never changes a basic species. Pigs will always be pigs, even though there are a good number of varieties of them. So far, and no further. No monkey has ever been seen to change to a human.

All of us are conscious of adaptation within species. It was Darwin's most brilliant discovery. Finches on the Galápagos Islands had different shaped beaks, adapted to the different conditions on each island. If there can be such changes in such a short space of time in isolated species, then surely the bigger picture of adaptation of an animal kind into another animal kind is possible? But no. It is not possible. Many have tried, but all have failed. The shape of the Galápagos finches' beaks in fact change up and down from year to year due to seasonal weather-related factors, but all remain finches.

We see differences in the horse kind - Carthorses, Shetlands, Arabs, zebras, and the closely related donkey. Many varieties, but still only horse. Boundaried within the kind. A horse and donkey mating produce a mule. But a mule cannot reproduce. So far and no further.

It is the same with the cat kind, the dog kind, the buck kind, the rose kind, the tulip kind, the daffodil kind and all the rest. Every kind. Many species, individual kinds. No amount of experiments to try to cross kinds to prove Evolution have had any success, or been justified by any observation. *Micro*evolution is observable and useable. *Macro*evolution just doesn't exist.

Truly one has to have enormous faith in the totality of Evolution to believe that one day someone is going to be consistently successful in mutating or adapting even one kind into another kind, to prove in some way that that was the norm billions of years ago into our ancient past. So far there is no evidence of it whatsoever, and it's not for the want of trying. And to have enormous faith that someone, somewhere, will find any link between kinds in the fossil record. So far there is not one, and billions are needed.

I laugh sometimes when I watch scientific programmes on TV. They say something like: "This creature had no eyes. It thought it ought to be able to see, so grew some over the years." What kind of nonsense is that? What creature knows what physical features it lacks? Fishes think they should have wings, so grow them? What fish even has the capacity to think like that anyway? Besides, what human, much less more unintelligent or primitive creatures, can select to have another feature? I think I should have wings! I could do with six fingers on each hand to enhance my piano-playing and computer keyboard skills. I can't even change my ability to pitch a note accurately. I think Jesus asked a sane question here: *"Which of you by worrying can add one cubit to his stature?"* (Matt 6:27 NKJV).

Yet intelligent men and women seriously think primitive creatures did that sort of thing - evolved and changed features of their own accord, or by a deteriorating mutation.

This is another reason why I think the rationale of Evolution is seriously flawed.

Fossils.

Many of you reading this might have already been asking the question: "Surely the fossils supply some missing links, don't they?" Well, the hunt for fossils has been enormous. Once sparked off, the fossil discovery has been prolific. Indeed, people have been hunting fossils for over 150 years, even from before Darwin's "The Origin of Species" of 1859. In all this, no one has found any links connecting any kind. There have been species of extinct creatures, all remarkable in their own right. But no missing links.

Here integrity comes in. Evolutionists are so desperate to find links that justify their theory that deliberate deception has emerged in many fields. Eohippus - the supposed link between horse and dog - has been proven to be bunk, the fossil finds being bones of a number of creatures spread over a large area, and relating more to the hyrax than a horse – more a Coney than a pony. George Gaylord Simpson, world's foremost evolutionary palaeontologist said, "The uniform, continuous transformation of Hyracotherium into Equus, so dear to the hearts of generations of textbook writers never happened in nature."[4] Simpson, after stating that nowhere in the world is there any trace of a fossil that would close the considerable gap between Hyracotherium ("Eohippus"), which evolutionists assume was the first horse, and its supposed ancestral order Condylarthra, goes on to say "This is true of all the thirty-two orders of mammals…and in no case is an approximately continuous sequence from one order to another known. In most cases the break is so sharp and the gap so large that the origin of the order is speculative and much disputed."[5]

Nebraska Man also - they invented this supposed missing link from the tooth of a pig! Piltdown man was the same - a hoax. Similarly, Ernst Haeckel (1834-1919). You might have seen his series of foetus pictures that make man look like he came from a fish? The photographs were all falsified. Let me quote Peter Bowler: "Ernst Haeckel, much like Herbert Spencer, was always quotable, even when wrong. Although best known for the famous statement "ontogeny recapitulates phylogeny" (definitions below), he also coined many words commonly used by biologists today, such as phylum, phylogeny, and ecology. The "law of recapitulation" has been discredited since the beginning of the twentieth century. Experimental morphologists and biologists have shown that there is not a one-to-one correspondence between phylogeny and ontogeny."[6] ("In biology, ontogeny is the embryonic development process of a certain species, and phylogeny a species' evolutionary history." The theory has been discredited in its absolute form. *Wikipedia under "Recapitulation Theory"*.)

One tries to believe that intelligent scientists are also people of integrity and honesty, and that they report back to the public empirical evidence of proven fact. All advances in science move forwards by theories based on observable facts, followed by experiments to test the theories. But in Evolution we find the "testing phase" skipped, and many propound theories *as* facts. Statements about evolution happening over millions of years are made with absolute certainty, but no such certainty exists because scientists cannot observe historical events. "Millions of years of change" cannot be repeated in a lab on a Monday afternoon. David Attenborough is famous for it. "Here we have a flower with a very long stem whose nectar can only be drunk by this one hummingbird with a very long beak. They live together and support each other in an eco-dependent environment." So far, excellent. Then the leap of faith. "Isn't it wonderful what Evolution has accomplished?"

Here we find a conflation of two arguments into one in order to pull the wool over people's eyes. What is evolution? On the one hand it leads to small changes such as different skin colour, or hair colour, or changes to the lengths of beaks and lengths of flowers, then Hey Presto!, with a slight-of-hand-trick, it can turn a bacterium into a man, all under this magical word "evolution." But what they fail to tell you is that the micro-evolutionary changes require only a change in the way *pre-existing* genes are expressed, the second idea of macro-evolution requires the writing of *new genetic information*, which is impossible without an intelligent author. And natural selection that gives small changes only mirrors what mankind has been doing in artificial selective breeding programmes anyway. Look at all the types of dog in the world from the Great Dane, to the Pug faced English Terriers to the Chihuahua, all bred by human beings from a small group of wolves. But no one has ever bred two dogs and got a cat, or seen a chicken hatch from a reptile's egg! While natural selection may be able to explain the size of beaks and flowers, it cannot explain the *origin* of either beaks or flowers because the whole system has to be there at once to function at all. They are irreducibly complex.

While I am onto this, let me tell you about a monkey experiment. The chimpanzee is apparently man's nearest relative in the evolutionary tree. So let me quote from an article by Nancy Darrall in Origins 42 of December 2005.

"In the 1990s, the research group at Yerkes Regional Primate Research Centre in Atlanta Georgia was continuing to work on language in primates. Sue Savage-Rumbaugh designed her experiments to avoid the errors of earlier programmes. A Bonobo ape, Kanzi, learnt a system of visible symbols and also manual signing during the day-to-day activities of life on a 50-acre parkland. Kanzi was in the company of researchers 7 days a week for at least 9 hours a day over a period of 3.5 years. By the end of this time, when Kanzi was six years old, researchers had recorded 12,691 utterances for analysis. The majority, 96%, of those utterances were requests which means that Kanzi did receive a reward 96% of the time, not in the usual sense of conditioning experiments, but by receipt of the requested item.

"It is perhaps a telling aspect of the work that most of those who have trained chimpanzees have refused all requests to share their raw data. (Pinker, 1994 page 337)[7]. It should be remembered that pigeons can be taught to press keys in a certain order to receive their reward, so, with no implied insult to Kanzi and his researchers for all that they accomplished, a "bird brain" is adequate for this level of communication! In addition, rather than ask the question about whether the Primate can learn the task, we need to consider whether it is the outcome of a similarity in neurology and cognition between ape and man or whether it was the result of training by competent language users teaching Kanzi learnt strings of words. Steven Pinker (1994)[8], discussing this research in his book "Language Instinct", concludes "deep down chimps just don't get it."

"So, is there any evidence of a smooth evolutionary progression from animal communication to human communication? Only humans, and only children at that, can master a first language without any specific instruction. Chimps need extensive training to gain a little. There is an enormous gap between chimps and humans in their capacity to learn and use vocabulary and in their ability to understand and use grammar. Even with the Herculean effort of trainers in various research projects with primates, the rate of learning words was vastly inferior to human infants, suggesting that quite different mechanisms are involved (Hauser *et al* 2002)[9]."[10]

So, cogent and careful research discovered two things: first, there is a huge gap between apes and humans in ability. Second, through the window of communication skills, there is no discernable connection between apes and humans in any supposed evolutionary tree.

Let's go back to fossils. There is a limitation in fossils. So let me explain how fossils happen. They have to be buried alive under tons of earth. The earth adjusts around their shape, the pressure eventually petrifies them, and the rock they form takes on the shape of the creature. It is so accurate that barbs on feathers on bird's wings are petrified exactly as they were on the bird, and there is one fossil of a large fish with its mouth wide open about to eat a smaller fish. Remarkable instant death. It has been shown that enough pressure can petrify a creature and make it into a fossil within weeks.

You will see immediately that normal animal deaths do not produce fossils. Take Africa. A zebra is killed by a lion. When he and his family have finished chomping, the hyenas and jackals have a chomp. Then the vultures and other carrion. Finally the ants and bugs pick it clean. It is the Lord's (some would call it Nature's) way of stopping disease spreading from rotting carcasses. I would say that it takes three days for a live animal to become a super clean skeleton. Then, after a few years the bones decay to dust. No fossils. For instance, I am given to understand that no one has ever found a fossil of a bison in America. Millions of bison. Not one fossil. Instead, all died and decayed to dust.

Therefore, if a missing link died a natural death in any other way than by being buried alive by tons of rubble, there will never be a fossil of it. Hence the limitation of fossils - there will never be a full account of every species of creature that has ever lived.

Why not? Tons of earth or rubble presupposes catastrophe. Obviously. Creatures which lived outside catastrophic periods like we do now, decayed into dust just like our bodies will.

Biblical creationists will immediately brighten up at that. Why? The Flood is the obvious catastrophe that springs to mind. It was global. It was sudden - 40 days of continuous rain followed by all the enormous floods and mudslides and so on. Did you know that there are a number of fossil fields in the world where hundreds of animals of many species are huddled together as if trying to avoid a disaster? They are huddling together in just the sort of way that cows and sheep do on a patch of high ground on the flood plains of Somerset after a week of winter rain.

Yet still there are no missing links found within the enormous fossil count. The chances of finding any now grows slimmer as the years go by. The chances that most of the fossils in this world were produced at much the same time is high. Why? Because we find recognisable creatures among the fossils - rhino, elephant, buck, buffalo and other creatures familiar to us. Of course, there are fossils of other creatures we don't recognise, and their catastrophe (like a volcanic eruption) could have occurred at a very different period in history. But still no empirical confirmation of the Theory of Evolution is found among the fossils. Not one.

Geology.

In order to get Darwin's billions of years for his biological evolution, he had to find those billions of years in the rocks. If it could be proven from the rocks that the earth was young, Evolution would die instantly.

So Darwin's contemporaries in Geology were James Hutton and Sir Charles Lyell. They were pro-active to find a rationale that justified Earth's longevity. Lyell found a cliff in France where the layers of rock were stratified, so he took samples from each layer and looked to find fossils in each stratum. Then he catalogued both the strata and the fossils. Taking Darwin's theory and assuming that the more primitive fossils belonged to an earlier era in a lower stratum, he guessed the age of the rock accordingly. Actually, he *invented* the ages. Because he and Darwin had a point to prove, they injected tens of millions of years into each stratum. So emerged the geological calendar, called the Geological Column. The Palaeozoic covers six sub-divisions of time, the Mesozoic covers three, and Archean, the earliest, covers four. The earliest two (Archean and Proterozoic) are often referred to as the Precambrian era. From Lyell's private letters we know that he conferred with Darwin and others to "free the science from Moses",[11] and over time the group dated the fossils from the rock strata, and the strata from the fossils. A circular argument. Almost incestuous! There was no proof for the ages of either the rocks or the fossils. Moreover, there were no other consistent and complete stratigraphic formations in the world that were the same as the original they found. The layers were (and are) in different orders, some eras were missing, and some strata contained the wrong fossils. There was no verification of any of the suggested era anywhere in the world. And why are there no fossils in Precambrian rocks? Indeed, there are fossilised polystrate (multi-stratum) trees standing *vertically* in horizontal sedimentary rock layers that, according to the geological table, took tens of millions of years to form. Impossible! I have a photo of one.

Nevertheless, despite the lack of empirical verification, the geological table has been accepted in the scientific world, not because it is accurate or justified, but because there is no other. At least they can call a rock by some kind of name now. Silly names too!

Again, it's the lack of integrity that troubles me. How can one believe in a philosophy when its very foundation is laced with deception? Have you noticed that when the gurus of Evolution are on thin ground, they revert to shouting louder, or making snide or critical personal attacks against those who disagree with them? Let me quote from Dr Paul Garner in his editorial to Origins 46. He is analysing a BBC programme on schools called Waterloo Road. "Throughout the episode, Christians who believe in creation were caricatured, ridiculed, belittled and generally portrayed as sinister, unscrupulous, manipulative, obnoxious, insensitive and crass." It's a common emotional tactic by all those who believe in their personal religious philosophy regardless of its perceived irrationality. (I used to do it myself in my early Christian days against other Christian denominations!) It is often used by religious zealots (Christians, Hindus and Muslims are typical current examples) who fight lopsidedly for their religious world view with all the emotional verve they can find, and even kill for it. I'll give evolutionists that credit - they may have lied, deceived and cheated to support their theoretical world view, but I've not yet heard of any of them killing.

So science had to find another way to date rocks.

Thus we move to dating methods. Michael Benton comments:

- "The best-known absolute dating technique is carbon-14 dating, which archaeologists prefer to use. However, the half-life of carbon-14 is only 5730 years, so the method cannot be used for materials older than about 70,000 years.

- Radiometric dating involves the use of isotope series, such as rubidium/strontium, thorium/lead, potassium/argon, argon/argon, or uranium/lead, all of which have very long half-lives, ranging from 0.7 to 48.6 billion years. Subtle differences in the relative proportions of the two isotopes can give good dates for rocks of any age."[12]

I recommend that everyone holds all these dates and all these methods lightly. They are ideas rather than facts, but scientists are coming to rely on them more and more because no one has yet found an alternative. It's a very inexact science, and research is still going on both from the creationist perspective and the evolutionary perspective to try to improve the quality of dating. Some of the dates are wildly inaccurate, like dating magma from a known volcanic eruption. The current research is a specialist discipline involving physics, mathematics, chemistry as well as Geology. The boundaries in this arena have not yet been established much less drawn. So hold all dates lightly.

It will be interesting to see what creationists come up with. How does one resolve a radio isotope with a half life decay period of a few million (billion?) years in a world that is only 10,000 years old? I have some ideas, but this is not my field. Just watch, and wait and see.

Cosmology.

I have dealt with the ages of stars in my earlier book. God joined the light of stars to the earth when He created them on day four (Genesis 1). They were designed to bring light to the earth, so that's what they did on the day they were created. Even some secular cosmologists now consider it a possibility that the speed of light was much faster in the past in order to overcome problems in the big bang theory.[13]

There are untold wonders and mysteries in the heavens. Cosmologists have a wonderful life (in my opinion) hunting for new treasures in the sky. I appreciate that much of their time is very routine searching, but it is still exciting stuff. I was almost alive when they discovered the planet Pluto, and am still alive to hear that they have downgraded it to a minor planet. And disappointed - but that is an emotional reaction not a scientific one! I watched Armstrong and Aldrin stepping out onto the Moon before the 1960's decade ended, and I have touched the (now very smooth) moon rock in the space centre at Houston, Texas. I've marvelled at the beautiful shapes and colours of galaxies and stardust taken from the (mended) Hubble Space telescope. I saw the photograph of a blank bit of sky that was casually left alone while the astronomers went on a Christmas break. It revealed a myriad of galaxies no one ever knew existed before so far away they looked like stars with very faint light. What a discovery! There are more intriguing things out there than man can ever dream of. I often dream of being a Space Explorer, but that's a pilot's dream. One day I will do it, but in a resurrection body that needs neither a space suit nor a space vehicle, and which is not restricted to the speed of light, or the need of oxygen.

The committee is out on Cosmology too. Does the red shift in the light spectrum from a star really indicate phenomenal speeds? Or does it indicate something different? Why don't the star constellations change shape if they are moving so fast? What is the real reason why the mathematics of space and matter don't tie up? Has the speed of light remained constant? How *exactly* does light travel through the vacuum of space? Is there other life out there in the cosmos – because there is still no evidence of any yet? There are many unsolved mysteries in the cosmos which will gradually be untangled as we move deeper into space and further along the timeline. But not yet. Nothing is proven.

So in the disciplines of Biology, Anthropology and Geology there has been deception in far too many issues, and Cosmology is such a young and a vast science that even basic problems have not yet been resolved.

More and more research has been conducted on many of the issues that Darwin assumed. Many, if not most of them have led scientists of integrity to question the validity of his basic thesis. It has taken a long time. But the century and a half of investigation has rewritten much of the data, the strength of Darwin's original arguments has been seriously eroded and it now lives on thin foundations. Moreover, the findings of scientists are being made more and more available for the average citizen to understand - when once we have mastered (some of) the specialist technical jargon that has been invented in every discipline. Thus some of the following tenets are either unproven or up for a different interpretation:

- The age of the rocks.
- The dating methods.
- The evolutionary tree, now virtually non-existent.
- The specific lack of any missing links between any kinds.
- The emerging impossibility of mutations producing anything good or consistent, and the preference of Nature towards limited adaptation.
- The incredible complexity of life in microscopic areas.

So let's look for a moment at that last one. Darwin had no facilities for investigating the workings of a cell. He called it a black box. Stuff went in one end and other stuff came out the other, and he didn't know how. But we do. Microbiologists have taken the lid off the black boxes and are still doing so. Inside a single cell there are very complex chemical and biological motors that process nourishment and waste in a beautiful and very efficient way. Michael Behe, a microbiologist, expresses this as "irreducible complexity".[14] Further research has revealed that even these mechanisms can be broken down and evaluated, but his description still stands. That is, the design of a cell cannot be reduced any more without it ceasing to function. The illustration that many use is of a simple mouse trap. The parts are simple and few. But every part is necessary for it to work, from the wooden base through to each staple. Remove one item and the whole device ceases to function. It is the same with a cell. Remove one little part and the cell stops functioning - irreducible complexity. It is as impossible for a cell to "evolve" as it is for a mouse trap. Both "appeared" as one functioning unit. Indeed, many are concluding that, in order to work at all, cells were as "designed" as mousetraps are.

So this is not an area in which evolutionary scientists can be deceitful. Straight scientific research is showing that there cannot possibly be any evolutionary progression in the functional development of life. That applies to plants and animals as well as man. "Life" cannot emerge spontaneously, or evolve over a period of time, however long that timeframe is extended. Life as we observe it (and therefore know it exists) appeared on earth from nowhere, separated into kinds (human, animal and vegetable) and we are left with a huge question mark as to where they all came from. The Evolutionary model is growing more and more empty of empirical justification. Consequently many scientists are turning to Intelligent Design as the only tenable origin of life.

I have already stated that the origins of life are lost in antiquity where no record exists - either in writing or in the rocks. Therefore much of it is guesswork, based on today's observed facts and extrapolated backwards. So whatever we believe on how it all began is a matter of faith.

Having stated that truth, the ongoing scientific research that fills the PhD theses is showing more and more evidence of design. The world we live in *works* - animal, vegetable, mineral, macro, micro and nano. It is also very beautiful. Spontaneous evolution from nothing (or even from matter from a Big Bang) is becoming more and more unjustifiable, and stretching the intelligent imagination of extreme faith to its very limits. What is observed all the way through creation is Design, and very intelligent Design at that. It *works*.

There is common sense involved in calling Nature Intelligent Design (ID). First, it is becoming more obvious, as I have said. Second, it does not delineate whose Intelligence is involved. There are a number of religions in this world which believe in a supernatural Creator. For science to select any particular one and say "This is the one" would be to muddy their waters, and turn scientific issues into a religious battleground. So not identifying which Intelligence designed the cosmos allows everyone to select the Intelligence they prefer. Thus scientific research can progress without diversion and people can be happy with the God of their preference. Very shrewd.

But it is a thin line, and very quickly begs the question as to which Intelligence out of the many on offer is involved.

Evolutionists are getting very upset about ID. Why? It places the origin of the universe in the hands of a Person. Evolution is completely atheistic - no God. The problem with a Being out there who is Intelligent (and far more intelligent than any of us human beings) is that it makes every one of us accountable to Someone other than ourselves. Self-centredness in man hates that. So, whichever Intelligence one supposes, accountability and judgement become inevitable. This is wonderful for all people of faith, but hell for all atheists, scientists or not. That's why evolutionists are getting upset and publicising as loud as they can when every crumb of evidence that could back up their atheism is uncovered. They are being confronted by scientists of equal calibre, knowledge and intelligence as themselves who do not blindly accept the Evolutionary world view of self-appointed atheistic gurus. Not only is their philosophy being challenged, but their trump card "Science says" is being laid bare. Science no longer says that. Evolution is a dying faith. G. K. Chesterton said, "If there was no God there would be no atheists." A USA car bumper sticker said: "If you don't believe in God, you better hope you're right."

In many areas of scientific research the committee is still out. Consequently there are still some fragments evolutionists can cling on to as they maintain their stance. But scientific research continues in all disciplines, pushing back the boundaries of knowledge. Most research deals with the current world in which we live, rather than its origins. Nevertheless, the content of organic life is proving to be very beautiful and extremely complex, however broad the research spectrum and however deep we delve into its functionality. Design is inescapably present and interlinked across the disciplines. In addition, the complexity is precise and perfect, right through the microscopic down to the quantum. The Being that designed life as we observe it has Intelligence greater than the whole universe, a care in designing that far exceeds any complexity man can produce, and a power that staggers man's most far-fetched imagination. How do living things have *Life*?

Select the Intelligence that you think best fits the description. Evolution is no longer a viable option in any form. ID is becoming the only viable possibility.

Over the last 1½ centuries of aggressive Evolutionary "evangelism", I have noticed that many biblical scholars have surrendered to its dogmas. Many have moved away from the unchanging revelation of scripture and have devised doctrines that, in various forms, have given deference to Evolution, like the gap theory, theistic evolution, pantheism, dualism and others. Some of these reject Genesis altogether. The rest compromise to try to bridge an unbridgeable gap between the Biblical Genesis and Evolution in a way that I think the scriptures describe as *"being blown about by every wind of Doctrine"* (Eph 4:14). Like the Vicar of Bray, (Simon Alleyn 1523-65) who changed his theology according to the changing political and religious climate of the Kings who reigned over him (look up the stanzas of his poem):

> *And this is law, I will maintain*
> *Unto my Dying Day, Sir.*
> *That whatsoever King may reign,*
> *I'll still be the Vicar of Bray, Sir!*

I admit it is very hard to stick with scripture without compromising in the face of such an onslaught of rationality and science emerging from specialist knowledge that we might have no handle on. Certainly, I used to be one of those who compromised. It was the only sensible and rational thing to do at that time. Silly me. It takes like to combat like - experts in Biology to challenge experts in Biology. It has been a dirty trick of Evolutionists to use narrow, limited specialist scientific knowledge wrapped in unintelligible specialist scientific language to justify a belief system. But at last they are being found out and being confronted by equal experts with a very different belief system. God has raised up scientists to show our generation that His unchanging revelation of origins is not just possible but probable. Hence Intelligent Design.

So, which Intelligence? You choose. But as for me and my family, we choose Jesus. *"He is the image of the invisible God, the firstborn over all creation. For by him all things were created: things in heaven and on earth, visible and invisible, whether thrones or powers or rulers or authorities; all things were created by him and for him. He is before all things, and in him all things hold together."* (Col 1:15-17)

NOTES:

I have deliberately tried to avoid dealing with scientific issues that are currently under dispute and debate. There is much research still going on, and many issues are still in the discovery stage. But we know enough facts now to decide whether Evolution is still a viable model of origins or not.

1 A. M. Sibley, *Restoring the Ethics of Creation*, Anno Mundi Books, Camberley, England, p.95, 2006

2 W. Dembski, *The Design Inference*, Cambridge University Press, 1998

3 A. Rendle Short, *Modern Discovery and the Bible*, IVF, p.77, 1957

4 G. G. Simpson, *Life Of The Past*, p.119, 1953

5 G. G. Simpson, *Tempo and Mode in Evolution*, p.105, 1944

6 P. J. Bowler, *Evolution: The History of an Idea*. University of California Press, Berkeley, 1989

7 S. Pinker, *Language Instincts*, p.337, 1994

8 Ibid.

9 M. D. Hauser, Chomsky, N., & Fitch W.T., The Faculty of Language: What is it, Who has it, and How did it evolve? *Science* **Vol 298**, no.5598 pp.1569-1579, 22nd Nov 2002

10 Nancy Darrall, Arguments for Design: Language and Communication, *Origins* **42**, Part 1, *Biblical Creation Society*, January 2005

11 Charles Lyell in private correspondence to Poulette Scrope, 1830. In: Lyell, C., (Ed. Mrs Lyell) *Life*, Vol 1, 1881. See also Charles Darwin in private correspondence to his son George, 1873. In: Himmelfarb, G., *Darwin and the Darwinian Revolution*, 1959.

12 M. Benton, *Fossil Record*, Internet 2006

13 Magueijo, J, *Faster than the Speed of Light*, William Heinemann, London, 2003.

14 M. Behe, *Darwin's Black Box*, Free press, 1996.

This Empty Creation.

I am told that we can get the total amount of matter in this universe on the head of a pin. Any reputable physicist should be able to confirm that. Matter is so small that it amounts to almost nothing. All the things we observe in the universe (as well as the things we don't observe) are held together by laws, which make them look big and solid. But "things" as we see them are nearly all space and nothing. Physics Professor Brian Cox gave this illustration: if we were to take one of the elements in the nucleus of an atom, say a proton, magnify it to the size of a man and stand it on the cliffs of Dover, its nearest electron would be somewhere in the north of France.

The elements themselves (protons, neutrons and electrons, and their smaller counterparts) are *all* that the matter of the universe consists of. I am amazed at the fact that everything we see and touch is made up of the same basic materials – just held together by the same laws, but in different quantities. The list of chemical elements is called The Periodic Table, and consists of 118 of them, with new combinations being manufactured and added all the time. Hydrogen is the first and smallest and consists of one proton /neutron in the nucleus with one electron buzzing round it. Ununoctium is the highest with an atomic number of 118. Hydrogen is a gas, others are solids (both at 0°C), but still consisting of the same basic elements. Of course, none of the things we see consists of one atom. Every substance is full of atoms, and the mixture brings us the variety that we know – from pizzas to stars, mozzies to cars. Because we know and are discovering the mathematics of this universe, we can now make all sorts of things, simply by mixing the substances together. For example, we have taken iron ore (Fe) and mixed it with carbon, manganese, chromium, vanadium and tungsten to make steel. Steel is a manufactured commodity – an alloy. So is plastic and all sorts of other substances – brick, concrete, tile, glass and all the rest.

But all are empty and hollow. We think they are solid. But that is an illusion. We think they are solid because *we* are made of the same substance – atoms. And our bodies are held together using the same mathematical laws that steel is made of. That's why we cannot penetrate the hollowness of steel or the hollowness of walls. The laws won't let us.

The laws themselves are also hollow. Mathematics is a *concept*, not a commodity. That does not mean that it has no power. The laws are real, but they are conceptual rather than substantial. Without them the elements would not hold together. But laws and mathematics, as we know, are invisible. We can write them down, but a written formula has no power to do anything. It is the invisible law itself which controls the elements that make this entire universe observable and solid. We can quantify the law of gravity and write down its formula (as Sir Isaac Newton first did), but it is gravity itself that operates. We can neither see the law nor its operation. But it still works (we are glad to say), because we can experience its effects. The Bible gives the illustration of wind: you can't see it, but you can know and feel its effect (John 3).

But it is not solid. It is only solid to our eyes, because our eyes are part of this universe's construction. As are our hands and feet. Our eyes and bodies are just as hollow and empty as steel and concrete.

Those (scientists) who study the mathematics and substance of this universe are, in fact, studying emptiness. That does not mean that the mathematics is unreal. It is certainly real. But all the mathematics and laws of this universe have been *created*.

This universe is a *creation*. It had a beginning, it has momentum – measured by time - and it will have an end. Even atheistic scientists accept that our universe had a beginning and will inevitably have an end. It is a *created* universe, which is why it is so hollow and so substance-less. Everything in it is, basically, empty. It cannot be the real thing.

God said he made the earth of dust. I presume that, when He got Moses to write it, man had not yet invented the words proton, neutron or electron. But either will do. Dust we are, and to dust we will return.

So, is there anything in this universe that is solid?

As I understand it, no. But there is a solid. But it is, and has to be, *outside* the universe that we live in and observe.

If this universe is created, then there must have been something, or someone, who devised it and dreamed it up. And that someone must exist outside this creation. There must be a realm that is infinitely greater than the universe we can observe if it, and He, is going to plan, design and manufacture a universe so complex and beautiful as the one we live in. It must be infinitely greater and more complex than the one we know in order to devise and get working all the laws that we do know. In the same way, man is greater than the things he creates.

But how come we have no handle on that other realm? To us *it* is hollow and without substance. Surely, we argue, *this* is the real and true realm? We call the other realm spirit or ghostly. Therefore, in all our experiences and calculations, without substance. We argue that if we cannot analyse or calculate something, it cannot exist. But that is a false premise. Can we, for example, analyse love? We can see and feel its effect. But what is *it* itself?

So now I have to turn to what can only be described as revelation. There is a Being outside our universe who calls Himself God. He claims reality and He claims He designed and made this universe. *"In the beginning, God created the heavens and the earth."* (Gen 1:1). We have no alternative than to accept that revelation or reject it. We have no proof for His existence other than what He has told us.

Why not? It seems, in His wisdom, that God has determined to hide Himself and all the realm of the Spirit from us. We have no handle on its existence or its mathematics. Therefore, in the mind of millions, it doesn't exist. People spend their lives totally absorbed in our realm, and are so caught up in it that they cannot stand back and see just how hollow and empty it is, or consider how it came about. As C.S. Lewis once wrote about liberal theologians' analyses of New Testament texts: "They claim to see fern-seed and can't see an elephant ten yards away in broad daylight." If once we acknowledge that we live in a creation, we have to acknowledge that there is a Creator. And then we have no alternative than to acknowledge His revelation of who He is.

The really difficult bit about acknowledging God's existence is to accept that we are accountable to Him for our very existence and, consequently, everything we have done with our lives. There is a judgement to come, standing alone in front of Him. He is responsible for everything He has made, including you and me. Therefore He has to call us to account for what we have done with this beautiful created body into which we are locked. Otherwise He could be accused of irresponsibility. That is the fundamental difficulty that mankind in general and most of us in particular do not want to face. Therefore it is easier to determine not to acknowledge Him and it in the first place.

So we stay locked in our hollow universe. So when we come to leave it (and leave it we most certainly will) we will remain hollow, substance-less and empty for all of eternity. We will suddenly know that there is a realm of the Spirit, that God really exists, that we are part of that realm (whether we like it or not), and that we have failed to accept the reality of the solid that we could not see. My

Bible says, *"Everything that is not of faith is sin."* (Rom 14:23b). So if we have no faith in God and His Kingdom, then sin and hollowness is all we have left. What a tragedy!

A casual look around this universe would confirm to us that there is something seriously wrong with it. It is bent. Tragedy and destruction, and issues that hinder life surround us on every side. Every news item is about disaster, and the very telling of it betrays a bent intelligence. Why do humans relish disaster so much? The God who created this universe says He is good. So where is that goodness? Natural disasters, diseases, man-made disasters and genocides flourish on every side, and all of us know that none of them are good. Indeed, it's only the natural creation that seems to be good in the midst of terrible tragedies and difficulties. Even that is not completely good. Animals eat other animals, and none of us really likes that. We accept it, and have far more acceptance of it than humans who kill humans just for the fun of it. At least animals kill for food, and not because they differ in world-views!

So why is this universe so bent? God tells us that it is us, mankind, who is directly to blame. And if we do not accept that, tomorrow's newspapers will tell of yet another human being who has done something appalling. Even you will do something today that you know to be wrong – or at least not good. Mankind has marred a wonderful creation, and, if I read my Bible correctly, it is mankind who will be the cause of its final downfall. Not the executor of the downfall, but the cause. Wickedness in man will cause God to bring the whole of this creation to an end.

But that is not the end of the story. Although God has restricted the initiatives of mankind from analysing the nature of the solid realm of the Spirit, man *can* access it. But only in a restricted way. That way has been laid out and boundaried by God Himself. It is only through a personal relationship with Him. That way He can control our access to the solid realm, and not allow us to get information that we should not know – much of which we will obviously automatically discover when we get there. Without that personal relationship with Him, we have no access at all, or we have only a bent access. There are creatures in the spirit realm whom we are forbidden to access, so anyone who tries is in serious trouble. They are bound to be wrong, or even catch something seriously wicked and catastrophic. Only God is good. No one else anywhere else compares.

However, if we gladly obey all the rules, come into a personal relationship with Him, God will enable us to access many of the forces and superior laws of His Kingdom. They will always be good. They will always have precedence over our creation. They can supersede any of the *created* laws that we are so familiar with, simply because it is the realm of the spirit that put together the universe that we know. The Kingdom of God rules over everything (Ps 145:13). And when we, in conjunction with God, use the realm of the Spirit to overcome disasters and difficulties in the created universe, then we can stop the bentness, slow down the difficulties, take authority over the disasters, prevent the wickednesses and bring light and life into dark situations.

Prayer is the place to start. Can God change a bad situation? Just ask Him. He nearly always will.

Taking authority in His name over bad things and people also works wonders. Wicked power-mad dictators can be stopped in their tracks. We can accelerate their demise on the authority of Jesus. Some are best out of this world to stop any more of their wickedness mushrooming.

So who is this God, and how can we access Him? His name is Jesus, and He chose to enter His own creation as a created being, just to show us how much superior the realm of the Spirit is to ours, to introduce us to His Father, and to enable us to know Him as He knew Him.

This Jesus healed sick people without medical training or knowledge. He walked on water, multiplied bread and fishes, and did all sorts of "miraculous" things that contravene the laws of this universe which we call Nature. He died by the hands of wicked men and did not resist them. Indeed, it was His death that cracked open the door to the Spirit realm for all mankind (if they choose to access it). Then He rose from death as He said He would. That is also miraculous. No one else has done that before or since. See - the Spirit realm has total priority over our realm. When God wants to use the very laws of our universe He has made, He does. That's called Providence. Why crash over them unnecessarily? But when there is no alternative, then the God of the Spirit realm releases goodness into our universe through "miracle".

Jesus is the demonstration that the Spirit realm exists, that God is alive and well throughout the universe (ours and His), that goodness can flourish and defeat wickedness, that the Kingdom of God has authority over everything, and that God will bring everything under His personal authority in the end.

"Therefore God exalted him (Jesus) to the highest place, and gave him the name that is above every name, that at the name of Jesus every knee should bow in heaven and on earth and under the earth, and every tongue confess that Jesus Christ is Lord to the glory of God the Father." (Phil 2:9-11).

So now go and change this bent and hollow universe into solid and good in the name of Jesus.

You can. With Him.

Design.

I hardly need to state the obvious that man is made for this environment. He is designed for this creation.

We live in it, we do all sorts of things with it, we control it, we use it, and we unravel it. There is no one else in this universe who controls this earth like man does. Angels don't. Animals don't. And, despite man's insatiable hunger to find extra-terrestrial life, there is no one else who does either.

Further, we disentangle and unpick it. We have chemists whose love is to delve into the how of things. We have mathematicians and physicists whose desire is to search deeper into the how and why of creation. Biologists unpick life in all its forms. And there are thousands of each discipline throughout the world whose *raison d'être* is to unearth even more information as to how and why. There is new information emerging from the scientists every day, and new devices being designed and made based on the discoveries from science they bring to us.

Man is inextricably involved in our earth and its environment. We live on earth inextricably involved.

Who else would do this? Who else could? No one.

For some to say that we are nobodies, phantoms passing through, and that we are insignificant as a species and have no destiny is utter nonsense. We have been designed to rule and develop earth's environment. And indeed, from the fact that we are discovering more and more things about it daily, we can only conclude that earth and its surroundings have themselves been designed, and designed for us to dissect. They were designed for us and the animals to live in, and we were designed to run it and disentangle it. We have barely started. For example, I am told that Taxonomists have so far catalogued only 10% of all the species of creature on the earth – birds, marine creatures, insects, mammals, reptiles, plants, bacteria and all the rest. "Taxonomy has been called 'The world's oldest profession'" (second only to prostitution, of course!) and has been dated back to 3000BC in China. Man is king of this creation.

But man is not king of the spirit realm. Indeed, despite many people trying to unearth parameters in the spirit realm, we have been singularly unable to access it. That it is there is undoubted. Every human being on earth has an instinct that there is a spirit realm, that it influences us, but that it keeps its distance and cannot be unravelled. There is no end to religions and religious people. Even atheists are religious - they believe in nothing. But it is still a faith. And they themselves desperately go on trying to persuade the rest of us that this creation "just happened" and that it had no Designer. But more and more mathematical certainties are emerging to tell both them and us that "mindless evolution" is in fact an impossibility.

The God of the Bible tells us that *"In the beginning God created the heavens and the earth."* I for one am very happy to accept that and move on (not fight it). But it means (and says) that the Lord of the spirit realm designed and made this realm we live in. So it must be infinitely greater (and I use the adverb carefully). It is also probably why we cannot access that realm; God is big enough and clever enough to stop us delving into it in the same way that we delve into earth – scientifically. But He has also put a curiosity into the hearts of all people as to what is "out there". We are inherently curious creatures. We are even inquisitive about the stars, and they are part of the creation we live in, but have great difficulty accessing. God has given us enough in the design of earth to satisfy our curiosity for every life time of every person who will ever live on earth. But He has restricted us from discovering what the design or details of the spirit realm are. There will be plenty of time for those discoveries when once we enter it after death.

But He has not kept us ignorant of it. It is there; it has its fascinations; but it is restricted. So what has God done to reveal it to us?

He has encapsulated the key to the knowledge of the whole of the spirit realm into one "thing". If we want to know what that realm is like, there is only one way to find it out. That "thing" is a Person, and He is called Jesus. He was a real human being just like us. He had little scientific understanding as we would understand it today, but He was and still is the only avenue to finding what goes on in that infinitely greater realm. He is the way to it. He is the Truth of it. He is the Life of it. He is, if you like, the very narrow channel through which sand passes through an egg-timer. He only is the access point.

Indeed, the Bible tells us that Jesus even designed and manufactured (actually created) this earth and its environs, that He will be the Judge of all its inhabitants, and that He will close this whole creation down when He has finished with it. He is the key to its very existence and its future. It even seems to me to be plausible that if we want to discover new things about *this* cosmos, then the best person to ask would be Him – the Designer and Manufacturer. But that is a diversion.

The down side of God putting the key to the spirit realm into the hands of a Being is that the only way to discover what goes on "out there" is to come into a personal relationship with Him. I can assure you that He is very approachable. But for those who do not want any relationship of any kind with someone others call God, it is a big difficulty.

Actually, it is more than a difficulty; it is a disaster. Those who develop a living relationship with Jesus while we have the opportunity here on earth will find that that spills over into the spirit realm after death. And if it is good down here, it will be even better "up there", where we are assured there will be no more sorrow, sin or sadness any more. Those who reject a living relationship with Jesus down here, will find that it is going to be very cold and lonely "out there" – mainly because "out there" is all Him. Earth's lifespan of three score years and ten hardly compares with eternity. To put all our eggs into earth's basket without considering heaven's basket is short sighted in the extreme. That's what I think anyway.

Design? We are certainly the best design for this environment of earth, and it for us.

But my Bible tells me that we are also designed for heaven and the spirit realm. That is probably why we have such a fascination about it. The promises that come through Jesus tell us that we will reign with Him in that realm for ever. We had no possibility of that ever happening if Jesus Himself had not cleared the way by removing the barrier of sin for us.

For those of us who are arrested and enthralled with the delights of discovery found here on earth, think much bigger than earth. There is another wonderful new realm "out there" that we cannot access "down here" but that we will only be able to access when once we get there. And then be enchanted by it for eternity. I have such sorrow for those brilliant people down here who will never be able to access the science of the spirit realm out there, simply because they are too proud to meet Jesus and surrender to His excellence down here.

But for us who know Him, it is good to know that we have been designed by Him. And, in my opinion, beautifully. We are fearfully and wonderfully, and, particularly, made.

Entropy.

Ken Pollard used to be a Physics teacher in a Secondary school. He now does DIY locally in Scunthorpe. I consider him famous for building and crashing his own aeroplane. He is a Trustee of the Peace and Hope Trust, working in Nicaragua with Mike Cole OBE, my friend.

Ken and I were installed together in my tent in a place called La Barra del Rio Grande, at the mouth of that large central river in Nicaragua that drains into the Atlantic/Caribbean. We were demolishing and rebuilding the clinic that had been constructed by the Government some 6 years earlier. I was casually remarking how quickly things deteriorate in the fierce tropical climate. He casually replied 'Entropy.' This started a useful conversation and Revelation I have never forgotten. It was Revelation to me because although I had heard of the word, I had no idea what it was or what it meant. He told me. It is the tendency of everything in the universe to decay and degrade to chaos. The dictionary definition is hopeless, so here is my friend Tony Langmead's: "In a closed system without an input of energy, disorder tends to increase. (That is, Entropy increases)." Entropy can only be slowed or stopped (but not for long) by the injection of energy. The scientific community has accepted that the whole universe is running down. Christians would add "to the disorder and chaos it was at the beginning".

This brought me to contemplate the amount of energy that God must have put in to change the chaos of Gen 1:2 to the order and beauty of Gen 1:31, where God saw what He had made and called it "very good". The atomic bomb would confirm to us that Einstein's formula $E=mc^2$ is correct. That says: Energy = mass multiplied by the square of the speed of light. That goes on to tell me that the energy God put into the creation must have been unbelievably phenomenal. Science knows no effect greater than its cause, so God must have energy much greater than the creation. If the present theories of cosmologists and physicists are correct, then our sun is a continuous chain reaction of nuclear fusion and fission. And, presumably, the billions of stars in our own Milky Way Galaxy, and the billions of galaxies in the universe are the same. The energy involved in all that creation is beyond our wildest dreams and way beyond our wildest calculations. How phenomenal therefore is God's restraint to hold Himself back toward us on this earth, enough to hide His immensity? But I digress. The original creation cannot have included entropy. That which was perfect in every respect cannot have incorporated a law which deteriorates everything to decay and chaos.

So when was Entropy created? Hmmm. I'm not convinced it was actually 'created'. It's a bit like evil. I wonder if evil is not merely an automatic opposite of good? That is, if good is absent, evil is inevitable, and takes the equal and opposite form of the good it replaces. So untruth is an inevitable opposite of truth. And deceit of integrity. Thus, if someone is not a person of integrity, they will automatically be deceitful. It cannot be avoided. I recognise that Is 45:7 quotes God as saying, "I create evil". But I wonder if what God actually created was opposites, such that everything in His creation was in balance? Like North and South poles of magnets? Or High and Low Pressures in Meteorology? But it's only a thought, and I wouldn't base an eternal doctrine on it. So let us return to the creation beginning.

So where did satan get his evil from? Isaiah 14 tells us exactly what happened to him; it is a succession of I, I, I, me, me, me. Ezekiel 28 tells us that he was "The Guardian Cherub," and admired his own beauty and capabilities causing him to "go solo" and set up his own empire to try to replace God's. The cherubim are fearsome creatures (see their description in the first 10 chapters of Ezekiel), and are guardians of God's Throne. Lucifer was the chief Cherub. So he was the greatest created spirit being in the universe. Fearsome. Where did his evil come from? Well, my view is that God is a Trinity, a family. And all good and godly things flow from togetherness, unity, oneness and family. So when someone breaks that unity and oneness and decides to "go it alone", the opposite of who the Trinity is, then the opposite of goodness kicks in. And because all the angels are perfect, then the opposite of goodness must have kicked in absolutely, instantaneously and perfectly with Lucifer, changing his name to devil – the accuser. One third of the angels thought he was wonderful and joined his rebellion against God, which indicates that they have choice like we do. So I think that satan "became" evil in a moment of time, transformed into The Devil instantaneously the moment he rejected God's perfect ways and "went solo".

So far so good.

So when did Entropy come in? I surmise it came in at Genesis 3, with the fall of Man.

But before I get there, I need to look at the authority structure God instigated on earth. It seems that God has placed an angelic being in charge of each heavenly body. He calls the host of heaven all by name, and calls the stars by name. He calls both stars and angels His Host, and each are named. I conclude that each star and each angel are interlinked. What is very clear is that satan is the heavenly being whom God put in charge of the earth. He is the *"Prince of the Power of the Air"*, and *"god of this world."* So God put His greatest created heavenly being in charge of His most important heavenly body – earth. Satan was supposed to be the liaison between man and God. According to Heb. 2, all angels are *"ministers to those who are to be heirs of salvation."* So man was designed to listen to satan and liaise with him.

Man, on the other hand, was given responsibility and rulership over the earth. He was to till the ground and subdue it. He was given rulership over the animals, and that is why God asked Adam to name them all. God placed two very special (and spiritual) Trees in the centre of the Garden of Eden. Those trees were spiritual and decided lifestyle, and were not for sustenance. The Tree of Life was one. The Tree of the Knowledge of Good and Evil was the other. God forbad Adam to eat the fruit of the Tree of the Knowledge of Good and Evil, and gave Adam the reason: *"In the day that you eat of it you will certainly die."* God gave Adam (and Eve) choice. If Adam was to eat that forbidden fruit, then death was inevitable. I put it that way because when they did eat it, they realised they were naked. That is, "other than perfectly good" kicked in automatically. As did guilt, and they hid from God. That is, death began to affect them immediately and automatically. It was an inevitable result of "non-goodness" and "other than family". Evil is the automatic antithesis of good.

Of course, satan deceived Eve. There is only one opposite to God and His (their) good lifestyle, and that is what both satan and man have embraced. Man loves wickedness and is addicted to disaster. So does satan. They both love it together. And that is what God calls "death". So, when God confronted Adam and Eve with their wrong choice, He also gave them all sorts of other restrictions: woman would be subject to man and would bear children in pain; man would till the ground in sweat; the ground would produce thorns and thistles so that work would be hard from then on. And because man had been given responsibility over earth, when he sinned he brought death into the whole area of his responsibility – that is, earth. So death entered earth. And this, I believe, is what the scientists call "Entropy". Everything tends to decay, death and chaos. And if I have read it right, man's choice of sin affected the whole cosmos; everything, all creation, is running down towards chaos. I guess because man is God's greatest created physical being, along with man goes all his choices. Certainly, all the problems on earth other than natural disasters are man-made. We humans are still responsible for earth, and God holds us accountable, not just for everything we individually do with our lives, but for the whole earth too. We are its boss. So having thought through that background, we now come to the really interesting bit.

The way to reduce Entropy is with the application of energy. So, cars and aircraft need to continue to burn fuel to keep going. If you take your foot off the accelerator the car slows down; Drag and friction = Entropy. You don't have to do anything at all for dust to accumulate on your mantelpiece – Entropy. But you have to inject energy regularly to clean it. And up at our La Barra clinic, termites eat away at wooden structures and the fierce sun and rain rust out the corrugated iron. I have seen it, and calculated that gap at 9 years – a very short space of time in the tropics. So, if we do nothing, death and decay are inevitable in everything we do and are. Even in our bodies Entropy is evident: we lose teeth, hair, vision, sound, muscular ability and power. God has said some important things against laziness and idleness. On the other hand, God has made us workers – even as He is a worker. He has given us food and drink and sleep to renew our energy, and He says that diligence receives a reward on this earth.

The story goes of a man wandering round a National Trust property. It was beautiful. He stopped at one of the gardeners and said, "Hasn't God made this garden beautifully?" The gardener tilted his cap back, rested his foot on his spade and said slowly. "To be shore, zur. But 'ee should 'a zeen it wen 'e 'ad it orl to 'isself." That's right. God gives us prolific abundance on this earth, but the partnership He has made with man is that man should subdue it into submission and bring it into order.

This applies to everyone in everything they are doing. From the humble maid dusting the furniture to the President of a nation – all are bringing order. Have you ever wondered why maids can never cease dusting the furniture, and Presidents never find final solutions to the difficulties they encounter either nationally or internationally? Entropy. Death, decay and chaos is the inevitable direction everything is travelling in, and doing nothing is the worst possible option. How we all long for a quiet life. "Eat, drink and be merry, for tomorrow we die." But if we take up that lifestyle, we will die a lot earlier than we expect or need to. Entropy can kill.

And now I've got dandruff! Entropy.

Have you ever thought how excellent Entropy is? If it wasn't for Entropy, we wouldn't have anything to do. The house your grandfather built has deteriorated enough to be rebuilt; the house your father left you has to be maintained or redecorated; every work on earth is altering and changing such that there is always more work to be done. Every new generation has work because Entropy has decayed the last generation's work. Or even yesterday's work. Isn't that good? How would we ever earn an income without Entropy?

So the next question to ask is: "Will Entropy ever come to an end?" You might as well ask: "Will sin and evil ever come to an end?" because they are interlinked. Well, the answer to both is a resounding "Yes!" When Jesus deals with sin once and for all, then the inevitable result is that Entropy will disappear. We know precisely when sin will be banished from the earth – at the Second Coming of Jesus. There Jesus will appear in the clouds of heaven in power and great glory, accompanied by all Christians who had previously died. Then both those and we who remain will receive resurrection bodies, all those who did not serve Jesus will be collecting a non-stop frying in a lake of burning sulphur (I hate even talking about it) and satan will be imprisoned in his bottomless pit. There will be no more sin for 1000 years, and Jesus will reign from Jerusalem with justice and righteousness. Now let me quote Rom. 8:21-23 *".. in hope that the creation itself will be liberated from its bondage to decay and brought into the glorious freedom of the children of God. We know that the whole creation has been groaning as in the pains of childbirth right up to the present time. Not only so, but we ourselves, who have the first fruits of the Spirit, groan inwardly as we wait eagerly for our adoption as sons, the redemption of our bodies."*

The whole creation groaning? Yes. The earth dislikes Entropy as much as we do (and we caused it!) The "adoption of the sons of God"? That's the moment we get an eternal, resurrection body. And the Creation? "Set free from its bondage to decay." There it is! Entropy gone for ever. It's true.

So, work hard, bring order, wait in confident expectation for that Day of Great Rejoicing to come, and hasten the day of the Lord. Work to get earth free from the chains we gave it.

Logos and Rhēma.

55

I apologise sincerely that as early as chapter 7 of this book I am trying to slide you into Greek. (I will try not to do it again). But if you can catch the Biblical difference between these two words, *Logos* and *Rhēma*, it will transform your life forever. Both words in Greek mean "Word".

Let me make it as simple as I can to start with. *Logos* generally refers to the WRITTEN word of God (as in the Bible). *Rhēma* always, exclusively and only translates as a SPOKEN word.

There is a vast chasm between the two. The chasm is this: No person on earth can understand God's *written* word except through God's *spoken* word. God only *talks* to us; He doesn't write to us. To put that unambiguously – only personal Revelation from the Holy Spirit to you will enable you to understand your Bible - or give you guidance.

You may not be familiar with Greek. Neither am I in any seriousness. But I commend even a cursory interest in it. Once you get to recognise its strange alphabet (ά = alpha, β = beta, γ = gamma etc), an interlinear New Testament can be a great help in evaluating Bible passages. Which leads me to today's Revelation. This one is pure Bible evaluation, and has been most helpful in bringing me Revelation and thereby understanding.

The interesting thing about Christianity is that God has decided to do it all Himself. That sounds selfish, but it's not; it's the only way it would work. God is a Trinity. The Father delegated creation to His Son, who now still controls the physical universe, *"upholding the universe by His (spoken) word of power."* (Hebrews 1:3). The Father also delegated the redemption of the world to His Son Jesus, who has now delegated the control of the earth to the Holy Spirit. They run the universe together, but submitted to each other in love.

The Christian life in human beings is being controlled moment by moment by the Holy Spirit. It is a *living* affair. The reason why God has to do it Himself is that none of the faculties or intelligences found in mankind are big enough, adequate enough or holy enough to make it work. Nor that of the angels either.

By this I am saying that man is totally incapable of pleasing God in any and every way, and that, on his own, man cannot do God's will. Whatever we do, however good and kind it may be, is never good enough for a complete and perfect God. (So it is important to stop trying).

But God did not give up on us. Our rebellion severed mankind from Him, but the redemption of Jesus has neutralised and reversed that rebellion, and opened the door to making God's original intention in making the universe actually to work. But no amount of Christianity in any human being makes it work. What does make it work is God the Holy Spirit prompting us on the inside. It still leaves us to hear and obey. But it is God Himself who is doing the prompting. There is no one else in the universe (not even the angels) who is good enough and complete enough to make it work. God is the only One who can actually accomplish it.

Bearing that in mind, let's look simply at God's communication system.

There are two ways, from man's perspective, in which God talks to us. But in reality there is only one.

The two ways are the Bible and the Holy Spirit. But it is important that we realise that it is only the Holy Spirit who prompts us. The Bible on its own does nothing.

Let me clarify that. The Bible is a book, written by human beings and read by human beings. If those who read it read it with their human minds in the same way that they read a novel or chemistry textbook, then the Bible is dead. It may tell us facts, but it does not, and cannot on its own bring us into a relationship with God. That is, it cannot bring life. The only way that it can bring life and open a doorway into heaven and God's kingdom is by the personal intervention of the Holy Spirit. Jesus said, *"The Spirit brings life. The flesh counts for nothing. The words that I speak to you are spirit and they are life"* (John 6:63).

There are far too many Christians who think that the Bible is a kind of magic book, and that it automatically contains life. It does not. Indeed, there are Christian preachers and teachers (of which I used to be one) who teach the Bible as if it automatically brought life, and teach it as if they were lecturing on geography. Only the Holy Spirit can speak out of the Bible in a way that changes us and burns eternal life into our hearts.

Now the Bible makes that very clear, and it comes in the form of these two Greek words (the original New Testament was written in Greek).

The two Greek words *Logos* and *Rhēma* mean Word (I will use the capital for clarity). But they mean and imply very different uses of Word. Let's start with *Logos*.

The word *Logos* is used 329 times in the New Testament. It is the general word for Word, and represents a written word, thought word, idea, spoken word, studied word, and covers all the uses of the word Word.

In English the word Logic and Logical comes from *Logos*, and the dual words Bio-logy, anthropo-logy, geo-logy and many more also do.

But the best and most significant use of this word *Logos* is by John in 1:1-14. *"In the beginning was the Word (Logos). And the Logos was with God, and the Logos was God. And the Logos was made flesh and lived among us, full of grace and truth".* I owe a debt to David Pawson for his superb analysis of this passage, which I heard many years ago on a tape. There was a certain Greek philosopher called Heraclites (540-480BC) who, particularly, utilised *Logos* in a specialist way to define individual scientific disciplines. For example, "The Final Word on Bios" (animal life) is to be found in the discipline of "bios – logos", that is, Biology.

John, knowing this background and inspired by the Holy Spirit, wrote of Jesus. He is THE ULTIMATE WORD on the Universe – all things were made by Him. He is *the* Ultimate Revelation of God – The *LOGOS* that experiences and describes God to the fullest extent, the *"express image of God"* (Col 1:15). By using *Logos*, Word, John is saying that Jesus is the full and final expression of all God was, is, and will be. There is nothing that Jesus *said* or *did* that will ever be contradicted in the universe, or superseded. He was the initial expression of God. He will be the final expression of God. He is The Word.

It also means that God's Words and God's actions are one and the same thing. What He *says* is what *happens*. He *spoke* the Creation into existence, through Jesus, and it happened. In addition Jesus *"holds all things together"* (Col 1:17). Please note it is in the Present Tense. That is, God does and is still doing it through Jesus.

Consequently, all actions in the created Cosmos were performed by Jesus, are being performed by Jesus and will be performed by Jesus. Because Jesus was the Creator Agent, He is responsible to God for the things He made. That's why Jesus had to be the Redeemer - He had to take responsibility for allowing sin into the world. His Father semi-abandoned Him on the cross - He alone had to be accountable for dealing with sin. And that is why Jesus will personally come again and put an end to wickedness on the earth because He is responsible for putting it right. 1 Cor 15:24-25 says *"Then the end will come, when he (Jesus) hands over the kingdom to God the Father after he has destroyed all dominion, authority and power. For he must reign until he has put all his enemies under his feet."*

John 1 says: *"In the beginning was the Logos. And the Logos was with God, and the Logos was God. And the Logos became flesh and lived among us, full of grace and truth."*

The Bible, being the Word of God, is also a *logos*, as the more general use of this Greek word Word. I need to ask the question: "What is the connection between *logos* as we would understand the Bible to be and *Logos* as we know Jesus to be?" Many people make them the same. They say Jesus is the Word of God, and the Bible is the Word of God; therefore they are the same. This would be error. Jesus is *far more* than the Bible. You will find Jesus throughout the Bible, as He said (John 5:39). But you will find Him in a million other places as well.

Logos is a multi-facetted word, has many applications, and bears fruitful study of the places it appears in the New Testament. Generally, we refer to it as the Written Word.

So now what is the difference between *Logos* and *Rhēma*? *Logos* is the general word for Word. *Rhēma* is absolutely exclusive; it means only one thing; that thing is A *Spoken* Word. It is always and only a spoken Word, nothing more and nothing less. We can see the exclusivity of it if we consider the English word derived from it – Rumour. That also is exclusively a spoken word.

A study of The Spoken Word *Rhēma* in the New Testament gives us vital clues to living the Christian Life, tying up especially with the word "Revelation".

I will pick out only a few of the important verses.

Firstly, the Bible is very clear that communication from God to man is by the *Spoken* Word, not any other kind. Not even the Written Word of the Bible itself. The Bible points always to the Living God who communicates through Living and Now words.

"It is written: 'Man does not live on bread alone, but on every word (rhēma) that comes from the mouth of God.'" (Matt 4:4).

"…for the one whom God has sent speaks the words (rhēma) of God, for God gives the Spirit without limit." (John 3:34).

"The Spirit gives life; the flesh counts for nothing. The words (rhēma) I have spoken to you are spirit and they are life." (John 6:63).

"Simon Peter answered him, "Lord, to whom shall we go? You have the words (rhēma) of eternal life." (John 6:68).

"He who belongs to God hears what God says (God's rhēma). The reason you do not hear is that you do not belong to God." (John 8:47).

"If you remain in me and my words (rhēma) remain in you, ask whatever you wish, and it will be given you." (John 15:7).

"For I gave them the words (rhēma) you gave me and they accepted them. They knew with certainty that I came from you, and they believed that you sent me." (John 17:8).

"But what does it say? "The word (rhēma) is near you; it is in your mouth and in your heart," that is, the word (rhēma) of faith we are proclaiming:" (Rom 10:8).

"Consequently, faith comes from hearing the message, and the message is heard through the word (rhēma) of Christ." (Rom 10:17).

"Take the helmet of salvation and the sword of the Spirit, which is the word (rhēma) of God." (Eph 6:17).

"The Son is the radiance of God's glory and the exact representation of his being, sustaining all things by his powerful word (rhēma)." (Heb 1:3).

"..but the word (rhēma) of the Lord stands forever." And this is the word (rhēma) that was preached to you." (1 Peter 1:25).

So how do we reconcile *logos* (the Written Word) and *rhēma* (the Spoken Word)? First we need to see that Life is not in the written word: it is in the spoken word only (John 6:63 above). Second, we need to see that the whole of the Bible was originally given as a *rhēma* word of God. *"Men spoke from God as they were carried along by the Holy Spirit."* (2 Peter 1). The authors, whether historians, poets, prophets or apostles, all heard God speak first, and then they wrote down what He told them to write. Those writings that were not

God-breathed (2 Tim 3:16) were eventually discarded as not being "inspired", and the final canon of scripture was confirmed in the Council of Carthage in 397AD. Thus we have the *logos* of the Bible.

But I have to say now, and I have already said it a number of times, that the *logos* of God as we describe the Bible to be is, in itself, lifeless. Dead. Or dormant. It came from a *rhēma*, but lost its life as man wrote it down and it became part of this earth. It has no life in itself. God has hidden Himself inside the Bible. It is only Jesus through the Holy Spirit who can bring it back to Life. He does this individually as a person reads it.

Let me differentiate from now on between the *logos* by calling it the *Written Word* and *rhēma* by calling it the *Spoken Word*.

So what brings it life? Only the *Spoken Word* of God. It is the *Spoken Word* that brings life – the flesh counts for nothing. So reading the *Written Word* with one's mind cannot bring life – as no doubt all of us have found throughout our Christian lives. The *Written Word* needs to be transformed back into *the Spoken Word* by the Holy Spirit as we read. Reading with our spirits rather than our minds brings life. When we do that, we will find that every single verse in scripture can be an avenue for God to speak anything He wants through it, applying it in the most versatile way. What many Christians fail to recognise is that they *need* the Holy Spirit to bring light and understanding through their Bibles. Nothing else will. The *Spoken Word* of God and Revelation are one and the same thing. They are Life because they come from a *living* God.

So we have a sequence of *Spoken Word, Written Word, Spoken Word. Spoken Word* to the authors, *Written Word* from the authors, and *Spoken Word* to us from the Holy Spirit as we read. That is how the Bible becomes an eternal book, bringing Life to any person in any century in the history of the earth.

Now I don't know how much your viewpoint of the Christian life has been changed by these scriptures. But mine certainly was as I studied them in time past. All the solid things that we have previously relied on to give us hope and expectation in our Christian lives (our Bibles, our fellowships and churches, our companionship with other Christians, our Pastors, Ministers and Leaders, our worship, the preaching, the counselling etc) do not in any way compare with the thing that seems to be most elusive to modern Christians: - the *Spoken Words* of God. Indeed, if we put our trust in any of those things mentioned, our Christianity will certainly die or become lifeless. Yet these Bible verses suggest that if we have those *Spoken Words*, hear them and obey them, we actually have the real goodies that Jesus came to give us. Without them, we actually have nothing – or maybe we just have mist.

May the *Written Logos* of God open up to you the most precious conduit and artery you can ever secure to obtain your full redemption – His *Spoken Rhēma* words.

The Human Being.

We all know who we are. Humans. But do we really know what a human is?

We see one another from the outside. We recognise each other because each one of us is unique. We have a unique body that is different from every other human being's body on earth. Indeed, no one has ever been like me from the foundation of the earth, nor ever will be. Or you.

Now that mankind has been able to expand the human genome, we see that the variety that is available to make any human is enormous. It is billions to one. Which is why every sperm is unique and every egg is unique. Thus the combination of one particular sperm and one particular egg produces another unique combination which is you and me. So far as I can see, the combinations are endless, verging on the infinite.

Our DNA is the measure of our uniqueness. That is why DNA is so good at identifying individuals in crime scenes. We leave traces of our uniqueness wherever we go. Our DNA has governed our bodies. Our shape, our face, our height, our gender, our gait, our weight, and everything physical about us is different from everyone else. That is how we manage to recognise each other by sight.

But for blind people the uniqueness is still there. All of us have different voices. The pitch, the cadence, the tone and the way we handle words is unique, and blind people can recognise us by our voices.

School teachers know that each child they teach is unique. We each have different abilities in the classrooms, and the education authorities who insist that we all get better at mathematics and English and science and all the rest are living in cloud cuckoo land. Some will never be good at mathematics. Some never at English. Some never at languages. The combination of talents that I have cannot be copied by you or anyone else. No one can replace me in my uniqueness. And I cannot replace my successors either. I have limitations that may infuriate you, but you employ me for my talents and capabilities, and have to handle my limitations with grace. It will be the same for my successor. Very often we want to change our employees because we have difficulty handling their limitations, and their replacement will certainly be better at those issues. But they come with their own baggage, and we may well find that the first one was much more preferable to the second. But only in retrospect. It is so throughout the world. Ruthless employers drive their employees to be like them – perfect in their own sight. But no one can be like them. They are on a lost cause. Head teachers want their staff to be driven by anxiety like they are. Business leaders want their staff to be perfectionists like them. Even some Pastors want their preachers to preach perfect sermons. All of which is folly.

So, not only is our body unique, but our soul is unique too. The inner me is special, as is the inner you. Indeed, it is the inner me that controls my external body. Because this body is unique and fixed for me only until it dies, you recognise me by both what it looks like from the outside as well as what the inner me asks it to do. I think it is very important for us to see that it is the inner me that does the driving. My body is a Thing. A living Thing, but still a Thing. It is me inside that tells it what to do at any one time. Those of us who have seen a dead body know that bodies are Things. Without the inner living person, they are lifeless. We bury or burn them.

As we get to know individuals, we start to recognise that it is the inner person with whom we are communicating. Initially we communicate with the body – on the outside. But as we develop a relationship, it is the inner person who becomes more important than the outer. We start to like their character, their humility, their genuine interest in us, their ability to bend to our wishes, and we find ourselves bending to theirs. Indeed, companionship is an internal thing, a locking together of souls that mutually builds each other up. There are some people who do not build me and others who do. The latter become friends, often for life. We come to trust them, rely on them, and together we help each other through the trials and difficulties of living on this earth. That is, indeed, the basis for marriage as well as for friendship.

But the thing that is important is that the real me is on the inside, not the outside.

I am not my body. I am me, on the inside of my body. C.S. Lewis said, "I do not *have* a soul. I *am* a soul. I *have* a body."

The vast majority of people who witness someone's death are convinced that it is only the outer person who has died, not the inner one. That is, the body has ceased to function, but the person you always knew and liked (or loved) has moved on. They did not die. They just changed locations. And that majority know by instinct that they will see their friend again some day – when they too have moved to that other location. John Brown's body may be moulding in the grave, but his soul has gone marching on. We all know this instinctively.

Even if we have a world view that thinks that this earth is the end of all things, and that there is nothing else afterwards, when we sit by the bedside of a close friend and watch them die, very few remain atheists. At those times we gain glimmers of a hope in a future beyond the grave that defies our philosophies. I speak for the majority of people.

But I do not speak for the Christian. A Christian has had a personal encounter with Jesus Christ on their inside. That is, someone from the other location, who has gone before us, returns to talk to us and becomes a personal friend. Those who have had this encounter find Jesus to be real, genuine, good, kind, helpful and the best that is on offer. There are witchy people who talk about communicating with people on the other side, but they do not have the credentials that Jesus has. There is always something dodgy about them. None of them are the genuine article. Only Jesus is.

Coming into that personal relationship is an internal thing. Jesus comes to me on my *inside* – into my soul. At the moment of contact, the inner me gets filled with His presence in joy. My burdens disappear. My worries and anxieties all vanish as does my fear. Jesus is really real, and His transformation on my inside is also real and greatly to be desired. Then as my relationship grows with Jesus, I find that all sorts of negatives, many of which I never knew I had accrued from my earlier life, all get brought to my attention to be dealt with. As each one is exposed and I follow Jesus' suggestion to get rid of it, He incorporates within me a replacement that is genuinely good, and from heaven. In this way I am *being* transformed on the inside into a much better person than the one Jesus encountered in the first place.

It does not take long for someone in whom Jesus lives to start to read other people on their insides. That is, we start to communicate with another person's soul, to read them from their insides. We not only gain friendship with their souls, read their characters in their souls, but then start to appreciate them from soul outwards.

This leads to a pattern by which we communicate with people from inside out. Once we used to communicate with others from outside in, a process by which we never really need to get involved with them at all. Christians are all too aware, as we all are, that we are influenced by our bodies and by other people's bodies. (Are they ugly? Are they fat? Would I like that person in my house? Do they stink? Bad breath? And so on). But more and more we by-pass their bodies and "belong" in their souls. There are many bodies belonging to other people that are welcoming, and many that are very off-putting. But Christians are not deceived by good-looking people, nor distanced by ugly people. If we can only read inside their souls, or read their hearts, we will discern whether they are beautiful inside or ugly inside – whether to be cultivated or kept at a distance. Some ugly people are beautiful inside. The classic example is the Elephant Man.

So let me try to tell you how we will relate to each other in heaven.

When the body dies, all that is left (albeit temporarily) are the soul and the spirit. (It's our spirit that locks us into the other location, because the other place is all spirit). So people are left without bodies. So they are all soul and spirit. That is, the genuine nature of who they are, the real them, is fully exposed with nowhere to hide. That may seem threatening to some, but a beautiful thing happens when a Christian dies. The inner me, my soul, is instantly perfected. All the Bible promises that I struggled to fulfil here on earth in this decaying body are instantly completed and I become instantly perfect and faultless. My soul becomes fully everything that it was uniquely designed and intended to be. There is no question of hiding – that is a feature of this earth. No one will want to hide any more. There will be no secrets. I will be fully, completely, joyfully, extravagantly me. And you will be fully, completely, joyfully, extravagantly you.

The glorious thing about heaven is the appreciation we will have for one another. I will still be unique, in that my character, although perfect, will still have its built-in inabilities. There will still be things I will be perfectly unable to do. But that is the joy of having you around. You and I together can accomplish great things in heaven because we have each other, and there will be no restrictions. We provide for each other what is lacking in the other. (How different is the concept of the non-Christian, who thinks that their perfection in heaven means that they will have every ability. They think they will be like God. Indeed, throughout their lives and on into eternity they *want* to be God).

The promise of the Bible is that the Bride of Christ will be one. *We* are the body of Christ and His bride. Not I, but we. I will never be complete without you. But you and I, along with all the other trillions of those Jesus has redeemed, will be one. One Body. One Bride.

It is very difficult, if not impossible, to discern exactly what it will be like, seated as I am in this restricted and imperfect world. I can only conjecture. But my conjecture is this: in the same way that Jesus is in His father, and we are in

Jesus, and Jesus is in us, we will be in each other (John 14:20). We will belong inside one another to such an extent that when one does something, we all do it together with the collected wisdom of the whole Body. We will be one. That does not mean that we each lose any of our individuality or uniqueness. But it does mean that we cannot live or work independently, any more than the Trinity can. We don't lose anything of ourselves. We gain by having each together. If I failed in heaven (which will be an impossibility), the whole body would suffer and become incomplete. The whole of heaven would become a failure. But that cannot happen because God will be in us and we will be in God all working in His New Heaven and New Earth doing amazing things from the position of the Godhead. God has kept those things secret up to this point in time. We can only dream, and, according to 1 Cor 2:9, we can never dream big enough, for *"No eye has seen, no ear has heard, no mind has conceived what God has prepared for those who love him."*

We will not be one Person, but we will be one Bride and one Body. And, I believe, living inside each other, with each one fully known, fully recognised, and fully relied on. That's going to make us very big, both individually and collectively, in every way.

On this earth, the only other person who can live *inside* us is Jesus. That is why we have to surrender our hearts (our inner souls, our inner Me's) to Him in the first place. If we were actually able to have another person living inside us, judgement would not be fair. Here on earth God has restricted us to being completely alone on our insides. Jesus and satan are the only two "beings" that have access to us inside. Judgement is based entirely on the decisions we make internally in regard to both – obedience to Jesus or yielding to satan's temptations. Neither of them can force us to follow them – it is all our choice. Judgement is therefore scrupulously fair and absolutely individual.

Without Jesus on our insides we would be for ever isolated and for ever alone. But with Him comes the promise of living inside with the rest of the cosmos, with all the angels and with all the redeemed. But not until we get to heaven. There we really will be One, belonging to each other *internally*, in the same way that we belong *externally* with others down here on earth. Isn't the prospect enormously wonderful?

One summer's day as I watched a cloud forming and changing over the sparkling sea, I felt the possibility, one day, of forming and shaping clouds from inside them, rather than shaping them from outside like a potter shapes clay. I believe this was a foretaste of what heaven and the new creation will be like – creating the new creation from *inside* with and on behalf of Jesus.

Let me try to summarise this revelation to me. Here on earth no one but Jesus can live with me inside me. And Jesus never forces me to make a decision for Him. He only makes suggestions, and therefore all directions that I give to my body are entirely mine. All decisions of faith form my character and, via the Judgement, determine my eternal destiny, and I remain isolated in that arrangement while in earth's school. Humility, submission and grace are attitudes I learn on earth for my approach to other people. They cannot live inside me, but I learn to submit to them on their outsides. But in heaven, those attitudes of humility, submission and grace will be perfected within me, so that, when the rest of the redeemed live *inside* me and I in them, I will never take authority over any of them. In the way that I am now learning to submit to Jesus inside and make Him Lord, I will be enabled to make everyone else Lord over me in heaven, with Jesus being King of Kings and Lord of Lords. That is the ultimate aim of unity and being One here on earth. In heaven, Oneness will be perfect for all the trillions of redeemed mankind, just like the Trinity have always been genuinely One.

I have not forgotten our bodies, and neither has God. When Jesus returns to earth (the certainty of which grows nearer every day), He will give to each of His people a new resurrection body. It's a spiritual body (if you can image such a thing). But it will enable each of us to be complete in ourselves, and then complete in each other. *"So it will be with the resurrection of the dead. The body that is sown in perishable, it is raised imperishable; it is sown in dishonour, it is raised in glory; it is sown in weakness, it is raised in power; it is sown a natural body, it is raised a spiritual body."* (1 Cor 15:42-44).

It is difficult to imagine how we can be inside one another when we've got a body. But then, we can barely imagine a spiritual body.

Do you see how all the seeds of heaven are being sown in us as we live on this earth? The daily communication, the reading of others inside, the reliance on others to complete what is lacking in us, the need for a body, the beginnings of oneness, the delight in and acceptance of others without a hidden agenda – and many more things – all these are snippets of the heavenly perfection and lifestyle that heaven consists of. Earth is the shadow land. Heaven, which looks very distant, unreal and vague from down here, is in fact the reality of the universe. It is earth that is vague and unreal. This is physically true. Apparently you can put all the actual material of the universe on the head of a pin!

By way of illustration, consider time. Everything we did yesterday has already disappeared. Only vestiges are left, and they will soon die. In heaven, where there is no time, all things will be Now and real and solid. God is going to burn up this earth and roll up the heavens like a scroll. This earth is just a picture of the real, a vague image of the delight and beauty of heaven and the new, real earth. Living here on this earth is school; none of us has graduated yet, and wont until we lose "this body of death." I have caught such a positive grasp of elements of the other side that I can't wait to get there.

So, what is a human being? He is the pinnacle of God's creative genius. He is the best that God could imagine and make. We are even greater than the angels. We are certainly greater than any other creature we observe on earth. But God designed us to be immeasurably greater than our wildest imaginations. But that greatness will only be completed in heaven, and never outside Jesus. For those outside Jesus, heaven would be hell. And their hell will be the most awful state of any of God's creatures. Man was created for greatness. We either reign over this universe with Jesus, or we become the greatest shame in the universe.

What a privilege it is to be a human being. It is a miracle that any of us are alive at all, much less having the body, abilities and skills that we have. That privilege will be fully granted one day soon when Jesus takes us home. In Jesus I will be me for ever, but delightedly united with you for ever as one.

Christmas.

Christmas. (Tune: The Ash Grove).

With wood and flower sleeping, and kind shepherds keeping
Their watch on the hill-tops and down in the vale.
No cattle are lowing, for quietude growing
Steals over the woodlands in Bethlehem's dale.
Tired men, their way bustling; cool wind the leaves rustling
Are all the ears hear yet in Bethlehem's street.
The dark night is hushing the citizens rushing
To lay their heads sleeping and rest their tired feet.

The shepherds are watching their sheep on the hillside
When Lo! The horizon with singing is filled.
A light and a dawning like sunshine at morning
And angels sing how God's Redeemer is willed.
"A child born of Mary. A Son, meek and lowly,
A cradle with oxen and asses and hay.
Go, see now this stranger, all warm in His manger
And worship your Saviour born for you today."

All children should love Him, and give their lives to Him,
For Jesus that baby has died for them all.
He loves more than pure gold both those young and those old
Who yield all they have and respond to his call.
For Jesus in glory still tells us the story
How those who will love Him will sing the great song.
All angels keep singing and wise men keep bringing
Their gold and possessions throughout ages long.

With wood and flowers sleeping and kind shepherds keeping
Their watch on the hilltops and down in the vale –
No cattle are lowing, for quietude growing
Steals over the woodlands in Bethlehem's dale.
For Joseph and Mary, so tired and so weary
The dark night is dawning fulfilling God's plan.
A cry from her new boy gave Mary her pure joy
Salvation and heaven to penitent man.

Age 33

Nature.

There is hardly one person, I would think, who will agree with everything I now have to write. Sceptics and scientists, please move to the next chapter and skip this one.

I was sitting at the front of the ferry that crosses Lake Nicaragua and admiring the scene. The wind was strong and the waves were big. Little ripples capped the waves as the boat heaved up and down and the foam flecked the dark green water as the wind stirred their tops. Blue, blue sky filled the heavens, interrupted here and there with fleecy cumulus, purified by the latent heat of evaporation, and the sun danced and sparkled in its reflected glory on the ever-moving waters. A tropical paradise indeed.

So, if the scriptures are true, and Jesus is upholding the universe with His word of power (Heb 1:3), then He was doing all that. He was and is in the wind, He was and is the water of life, He was and is all colours and cloud and hill and grass and everything that constitutes Nature. He is Nature.

So why then is Nature so consistent? Why are there laws that scientists and the rest of us can utterly rely on? Surely the laws are laws, aren't they? We have a good handle on most of their mathematics. Indeed, Nature is so consistent that we can all do without God. We can rely totally on our own resources to live and survive earth. Millions do, and have done for millennia. They have passed on and left their philosophies behind so that, they hoped, we would all benefit from their discoveries. What if they were themselves duped?

There is a stark contrast between what the average person thinks and what the Bible says. But let me go on with the Bible logic.

If Jesus is the beginning, the middle and the end of all things, and if He is upholding the universe by His word of power, then I have got to be consistent and follow that statement through.

So, start at the microscopic. Every atom is "being" held together by Jesus. Even physicists do not actually (yet) know what holds an atom together. It has to start there. I have written earlier that this universe is empty, basically space. The amount of actual matter is remarkably small, and things are being held together by laws. So Jesus must also be law. Not just moral law, but physical, chemical and mathematical law as well. Gravity works, not because of its innate attraction, but because Jesus made it so, and continues to make it so. It is consistent because that is Jesus' character. Reliable. Faithful. Dependable.

If I have difficulty (and I would think everyone has) imagining billions of light years in billions of quantities of the stars, I will also have difficulty imagining someone holding together all matter at the microscopic level all at the same time. The only thing that we can compare the universe with is ourselves. And, in the light of the immensity of it all, we are pathetically limited and ridiculously small. It is hardly surprising that people are unable to consider a God *that* big. And even harder to think that the Jesus of the New Testament is actually the same person who designed it, put it together, is upholding it all together all at the same time, and is the Judge of all the earth. After all, on earth He was as limited as I am, wasn't He? Certainly. It is very hard to consider a man just like us who was God and has since returned to His original enormity. If the enormity of the microscopic and the enormity of the cosmos are beyond our imagination, then it is difficult for us to stretch faith into believing a God that big that far. I sympathise. But I will not retreat.

So what about the natural disasters? Well, we all know, or should, that the heavens have an enemy and a band of renegades. They are out to do harm to everyone and everything. They are unable to do anything without God's permission (of course), but they are pressing Him all the time, and He allows their silly stuff to continue because He already has a multiplicity of solutions that the enemy knows nothing about and will apply them appropriately and on time.

Then my thoughts turned to living things.

Plants first. It seems natural that if you plant a seed it will grow into its appropriate tree or bush. But hold on. Every plant has its own seed, boundaried in its DNA to its mother. You can't get an apple from a carrot seed. Ever. And God put those boundaries into every plant from the beginning. Of course, every cedar tree differs from other cedar trees in their shape and size, and I put that down to God's immense flexibility too. Everything living is controlled by The Life of the universe. It's not just the variety of living things that staggers us; it's the difference in each individual version of the same plant that is mind-boggling. Someone called it the wastefulness of creation.

That is not the end. Animals are living too, and their variety and differences are the same as that of plants. We all know that every dog has a unique personality, as does every parrot, chicken, cat and cow. They all have the same character DNA as their mothers, but they differ from them to the same degree. As do humans.

But surely, I thought, each animal and man have choice, don't they? Certainly. But the choice that God has given to all living and moving things is boundaried. So Jesus is still making sure that the beautiful body of our favourite pig works well. Its digestive system is completely out of its control, as is its breathing. Pigs don't even consider such difficulties – they just live. But boundaried. Pigs can't fly. Indeed, every living thing is moving around in its own bubble. Inside that bubble it has choice – insect, bird, fish, animal and man. Outside that bubble it cannot go.

So, the choices that every living and moving thing has inside their own bubbles are outside the control of Jesus. I am in my own hands inside my limitations. But because Jesus has limited the bubbles, He can handle those choices, blend every creature with each other and fit them into His plan for the universe.

So in all this, God has been very good to living creatures. He has not brought them under His microscopic control (although He keeps them alive in a thousand ways they know nothing about), but has given them flexibility and choice inside boundaries. Isn't it so good that we can choose to go to the Bahamas for a holiday? Pigs can't.

Where God through Jesus is in total control of absolutely everything, by His grace He has allowed His creation to do things outside His control. He doesn't mind whether we turn right, left or go straight ahead. He would wish we did what He wants us to do, because doing what He wants us to do is by far the most perfect thing to do anyway, and, when earth has gone and the newly created heavens and earth are the only things in existence, we will find that selecting His choices for us will have reserved for us a great weight of glory (as the Apostle Paul put it). God is always right (that's part of the Trinity's nature) and always has the best suggestions to make if we want to do right too.

So my thoughts turned to this world in which we live.

I in my bubble am influenced by any other of the living and moving creatures from inside their bubbles. I am influenced if a dog tries to bite my legs. In an extraordinary way I remain unique in my personal being, but can be influenced by all other beings. By my choice, of course. But if people are not aware of the infinite control of Jesus inside the earth, their bodies and their situations, they form ways of operating of their own. We call those World Views. Political, Economic and Religious. The influence others have on us outside of Jesus is enormous, so they form Political Parties, they surrender to Economic philosophies, and they follow Religious majorities (like communism, democracy, evolution, fascism and now Islam). But all these are man made. Those who are blind to Jesus and do not know that He is Nature, live in houses of mist. World Politics, Economics and Religions are empty mists. Have you noticed how intertwined they are? You cannot do Politics without being a World Economist and both are dependent on your World View. That is, your religion.

Those who think Nature is natural (that it just so happened and all the laws that govern it just appeared from nowhere), and have not seen that Jesus is Lord over everything, are seriously blind. They are as fragile and empty as mist themselves, lining up with all their choices and philosophies of mist.

But if Jesus is in all of nature and actually *is* Nature, then … You finish that sentence.

Showers, and Water.

I was taking my early morning shower today, and, of course, I started to ponder with Jesus. I just love showers. My wife Eileen prefers a cup of tea in the morning, and I respect that – and regularly make one for her.

But I like showers. This morning I reflected on what a delight a nice hot shower is for me. I have enjoyed them throughout my life, but today, I asked why.

How amazing that I have skin all over my body. It is not permeable to water. I can let the water course down my body and none of it penetrates inside the skin. How amazing is that combination of gifts and designs from the Lord? In addition, God did not design my skin like a raincoat – without feelings. He designed it so that every cell should be connected to my nervous system, so that the warm water would be felt all the way down my back, and front, and head, and legs and feet. All over, I could treasure pleasure. Just standing there (or lying in a bath), I could soak lazily, relax, and feel warm, cosy and cossetted all over. It is pure indulgence, I know. Few other people would make such a fuss over it. But I love it – as no doubt most of you readers will too. God made this body for pleasure. Wasn't that so very kind of Him? He surely knew that many of us would really enjoy a warm shower or bath in the morning or evening, and He specially gave us the ability to do so. In Nicaragua, which is tropical with an average daily temperature of 34°C all the year round, I take a shower at both ends of the day. Or a swim in the fresh-water lake.

C.S. Lewis, in his Screwtape Letters, described the disgust that demons felt at the hedonism of God. God loves pleasure, and He loves giving it to His creatures. Taste is another delightful pleasure. So are feelings and touch. Even cats and dogs love to be stroked! And lions love basking in the sunshine and having a siesta after they have had a good meal. (As do I after lunch. And I am delighted to say so and to have one). This earth is designed so beautifully that pleasure is incorporated in it from inside. God has given us all things richly to enjoy, so says my Bible (1 Tim 6:17). And there are eternal pleasures at God's right hand (Psalm 16:11). It is easy to think like a demon, and despise or reject pleasure.

But often that is a reaction to over-indulgence. People who disapprove of over-indulgence of pleasure often turn to the other extreme and take no pleasure in anything – just to demonstrate to the wanton that taking too much pleasure is wicked. But most of those turn out to be such miserable people themselves. David Watson once said, "The answer to misuse is not disuse, but right use." Christian people do not live for pleasure – they live for Jesus. It is His delight to reward us, not just with pleasure as a gift, but with the appreciation of it as well. *God* gives pleasure. Let us appreciate Him for all His goodness and gladness.

Showers need water. Somewhere in my writings I have talked about water, but I would like to add to that here. Water was the first thing God made on the earth after He made the solid bits underneath – rocks and such like. On day One of the creation God said: "Let there be light". And, of course, the whole electromagnetic spectrum sprang into being. But before that, as part of earth's incorporated necessity, was water. The whole earth was flooded, and covered with water. Earth and water belong together as One Thing. It was the first chemical God designed, and, if you like, it is the founding chemical, incorporating many qualities found in no other (just like the parable of the Sower is the founding parable of all Jesus' parables (Mark 4:13)). It was and is a remarkable chemical. Few if any other chemicals (about which I have little knowledge, not being a chemist) have their three forms close to room temperature. We use its liquid form, its solid form and its gas form daily. (What would my Eileen do without her cup of tea in the morning)? How come that chemical is made from two gases, oxygen and hydrogen? How many other chemical "solids" are made from gases?

I, being a pilot, have studied meteorology, clouds being one of my delights. Air can happen in bubbles (did you know that)? A bubble of air is surrounded with a kind of light meniscus, so that their temperature and humidity, their content, is loosely screened from the surrounding air next door to it. So when the hot sun warms the earth, one bubble of air gets hotter than its environment, and hot air rises. So up it goes like a balloon compared to its neighbours. Then its temperature drops (because it expands and stretches), but still rises until the water vapour inside it gets to a temperature when it condenses. Pop goes the water and cloud appears. Then something funny happens to it, because water contains a property that is called latent heat. When it changes from water vapour to water (gas to liquid) it lets off heat. Perhaps you can see it better if I give you some numbers? A bubble of air loses temperature as it rises at 3°C per 1000 feet. A condensed (cloudy) bubble of air rises at 1.5°C per 1000 feet (that extra temperature being produced by the latent heat being released). Hence, in the summer, you can see that the bottoms of cumulus clouds are all at the same level. That is the level at which the temperature of the air condenses. So far so good.

If the outside temperature is such that the bubble of air keeps on going up, and faster after the water has condensed, then it could go right up to the tropopause at about 36,000 feet, creating huge thunderstorms. The whole thing would be filled with cloud. And the speed of rising could be quite rapid – regularly generating lightning and thunder. Isn't that so exciting? But when the temperature inside the bubble reaches the same temperature as its environment, the bubble stops rising. That determines the cloud tops. What an incredible design water is.

Latent heat works the other way round too. When a drop of water evaporates, it needs extra heat to do it. So it steals heat from the surface it is on to do so. If that surface is your body, that spot gets cold compared to its neighbour. Try having a shower and not drying; the places where water still sits get cold quickly, the water grabbing heat from your body to evaporate. Hand driers in public toilets use heat to evaporate the water, rather than allowing the latent heat to steal it from your hands and making your hands cold. After a shower, a good rub down with a warm towel is part of its pleasure, and saves those little areas of chill as the water evaporates off your body.

Rain needs tiny nuclei round which the water vapour can collect and condense. That is normally a dust particle. Every drop of rain has a solid nucleus, even drizzle. Rain was not part of the original creation, and there is no mention of it in the Bible until The Flood. The same is true of wind. The earth was watered from springs, streams and rivers, and dew in the mornings. The whole earth was, before The Flood, one huge high-pressure area, the temperature at the poles being the same as the tropics. This is why there are many coal and oil seams of tropical forest (fossil fuels) in what are now tundra or arctic regions. The whole meteorological system of earth was radically altered during The Flood, and we now experience changing high and low pressure areas coursing across the globe in the atmosphere, the boundaries of which give us the lift up of cloud that produces most of the rain we need. Only God could think of watering the earth with tiny drops of water. It is very effective – isn't it?

Snow crystals are all six-sided or six-pointed. Hexagons. And all (I am told) differ from each other. Isn't that extraordinary? Have you ever studied frost on a bench in an early winter's morning? Frost and snow are all still water – but just more beautiful expressions of it.

God gives us everything richly to enjoy - I repeat it. He gives sunshine and rain for the pleasure of the good and the bad of earth, whether they acknowledge His generosity or not. Earth's pleasures are multiplied enormously by saying "Thank you" to the Good God whose pleasure it is to give you the pleasures you can measure and treasure.

The Unique Individual.

Surely God must have some favourites? But no. (Rom 2:11). He loves all of us the same. How does He do that? We humans find that very difficult, and parents sometimes love one child more than another. Isaac loved Esau, and Rebecca loved Jacob. But God loved them both. Mind you, He had a different purpose for them both, but His love remained consistently even.

Now it may surprise you to know that I have discovered how God does it, and put it into practice regularly.

So how does He do it? How does He love us all fully the same?

He loves us one by one.

He loves me fully, perfectly, completely as if I were the only human being ever born. In fact, I am: there has never been another person like me in the history of the universe. He loves you in the same way, and every other human being ever born.

He and I can do that because people are all unique individuals. There never have been two humans the same. Our talents are different, as are our limitations. Our DNA is unique, as are our fingerprints, the construction of our eyes, our characters, our personalities, our looks, our attitudes, the things that worry us, the things that please us, our desires, our food preferences, our vulnerabilities, our stamina, our feelings, the things that annoy us or frustrate us, our skills of hand or mind, the different ways in which we deal with the same situations and so on. Truly we are unique. No one really feels like we feel. No one else has the same perspective on life that I do, or on the now situation as I do. Or as you do. The kaleidoscope through which we each view life has a different pattern from that of everyone else. There is no such thing as a conventional human being.

That is how we can appreciate one another.

Look at how other people's skills bless my life. I like Beethoven's music, although I could never compose music like that. I like other people's art, sculpture, books, and paintings. I buy little artefacts to decorate our mantelpiece because someone else's perspective on life, which made them make that artefact as they did, enriches my life and blesses me. Someone else designed and made the car I drive – a fact that pleases both me and my family, and one that I could never have designed or built myself. I have a million limitations. Hopefully, I provide a smidgen of blessing to others through my unique character in the same way that others bless me. But my uniqueness does not in any way clash with yours. I am in no rivalry with any other human being. I am unique. And I enjoy my uniqueness so that I can bless others, and rejoice that you are also around so that I may enjoy your uniqueness too. You bless me simply by being you. Wonderful, brilliant, individual, abnormal, unconventional you. You are wonderful. And you are wonderful not simply because you are a human being, but because there is not and there never has been another human being like you in the history of the universe. What a privilege for me that you are around during my time on earth. "Welcome to my world" Louis Armstrong sang. How could I possibly live without all the contributions that you and others make to my life?

God has so designed everyone in their uniqueness so that, together, we may enjoy everything that God has got for us to enjoy in this world. Without each other, and without each other's contribution to this earth, what would there be left to enjoy? There would be only God and His creation. That would be wonderful and, indeed, perfect, but Adam, who was the only person to whom that condition applied, got lonely quite quickly. He needed another human being, and got Eve. Then he got the rest of mankind. God has designed man to love other people and to belong to one another. If we could possibly envisage it, how wonderful it would be to know everyone else and appreciate the uniqueness that each one brings to life on earth. As a species, we are one Being together, although we are very limited in ourselves individually. May I suggest that, if we could possibly combine all the talents and personalities of every human being into One Being, wouldn't we be truly amazing and truly powerful? Indeed, super-super-super-Superman.

God has exactly that in mind – but we all have to wait for heaven for it to be accomplished.

Now I can love and fully appreciate you simply because you are unique. I will never meet another human being in my whole existence that comes anywhere near to you with your combination of talents and qualities. I have enough appreciation inside me to enable me to appreciate you fully.

God, who is much better at loving people than I am, does the same. He loves everyone in just the same way and to the fullest extent simply because there is no one else in the universe just like each one of us. He loves us uniquely. And perfectly.

But with God there is so much more. We live in His creation. He designed it the way it is, and there is no other. It hangs together perfectly, because He, the designer, is perfect and complete in everything He is and does.

So let's take you. God has designed the DNA molecule to be so enormous and so complex that the combinations of DNA that are possible are infinite. That enables you to be unique. (As a matter of interest, that also applies to the DNA of every animal and insect, and of every tree and shrub; all are unique because all have individual DNAs). A woman has, on average, 900 eggs with which she is born, all of which have different DNAs to make another human being. Every man pumps out, on average, "many millions" of sperm at any one go, each one having a different DNA. The chances of one particular egg and one particular sperm combining to make you are therefore, on average, verging on the infinite. The timing also has to be perfect. To have made you there is only one egg and only one sperm that will do, and only one moment in time. From a human perspective, the odds of you turning out to be who you are completely random and humanly utterly unpredictable. One scientist estimated the permutations at about 1 in $10^{1,300,000}$. This I have mentioned before, but it is worth repeating.

But my Bible says that God has known us and chosen us from before the foundation of the earth (Eph 1:4). So, from God's point of view, that is not at all random – it is designed, planned, organised and specifically directed. For the Bible to have a correct perspective on this matter, the only conclusion we can come to is that God has selected the egg, the individual sperm and the exact timing of your conception.

Consequently, I can rightly maintain that every conception is divinely arranged. There are no "mistakes". There are no errors. I also maintain that the moment that a human is conceived, he/she is an eternal being, fully known to God and impossible to destroy. (That's one reason why I hate abortion).

We all know that there are many couples who cannot conceive. God knows when every couple has sex, and He arranges every conception, so that His heaven may be filled with exactly the right people with exactly the right combinations of characteristics that together form Jesus' Bride. Did you know that all three Biblical patriarchs, Abraham, Isaac and Jacob had to pray for their wives to conceive (Jacob with Rachel to produce Joseph)? Their children were miracle children, but each one was the exact special one that God needed at that time. So we can see from the Bible, and also from our own experience, that every conception is planned by God. He has His hand on every one of us.

So let's go back to you. Why has God designed and chosen you to be who you are?

He has the long-term view. He has His heaven in mind. He has designed you to fit in exactly the right place in His heaven, and in the Bride of Christ that can be filled by no other. Your uniqueness, so clearly seen on earth, is designed for a specific place and a specific task in heaven. So walk cautiously on earth, and with prudence. This life on earth is not the end, not the final goal. Walk with heaven in mind. Carry God's long-term view with you every day. How easy it is to get so deeply involved in this world (pleasure, sex, ambition, self-satisfaction, career, greed, resentment, revenge, money spring to mind) that we fail to plan for heaven and, indeed, miss every opportunity by being too caught up with too many other and lesser things. Jesus, in the parable of the sower, described the thorns that choke the word of God inside us as *"...the worries of this life, the deceitfulness of wealth, and the desires (lust) for other things"* (Mark 4:19).

God has also perfectly designed the environment and tasks that will hone you for heaven, and equip you for heaven. The talents that you have been born with enable you to take a unique pathway through your life. That pathway will be the perfect location to rid you of the selfishnesses that you were born with, and equip you with God's characteristics. Indeed, exactly where you are is the best place in your history for you to meet with the Lord and collect His treasures as you pass by.

So the discipline of the Lord for you is to expose your selfishnesses, greed, wickednesses, lusts, and all the rest of the trappings of satan that you were born with and had started to develop before Jesus met you for the first time. He exposes them one by one so that He can surgically remove them, and replace each one with things like humility, patience, kindness, generosity, forgiveness, grace, magnanimity, courtesy and all sorts of other Godly characteristics that fit best in God's heaven. And the place where you are at the moment – in your home, at work, at play – is exactly the right place for you to be to learn these things. *"For we are God's workmanship, created in Christ Jesus to do good works, which God prepared in advance for us to do."* (Eph 2:10). God makes no mistakes – ever. Not even with where you are and what you do in every moment of time.

So what about the choices you make? You know, as we all do, that we make many bad choices. They lead us into trouble at every step. Do not be anxious about any of them. First, God has arranged forgiveness for each one – which we actually have to access. That is, ask Him for it. From the moment of forgiveness, God weaves our mistakes into the pattern of our lives. He turns every error into good, so that great grace may prevail in our life and the road onwards will turn out to be the very best possible and will be filled with every kind of goodness and blessing. God is correcting the deviations all the time and steering us towards His goal of perfectly equipping us for heaven. Even though the pathway that God planned is deviated by our sins, the pathway that results is the rich tapestry that is eternally me, rewoven by God's love and grace into what I will eternally always be.

The things that we do on earth – the job, the kids, the career, the money we accrue – all of these things are irrelevant in themselves. They only form a very loose framework round which the Lord designs and equips us for our place in the Bride of Christ. The things we accomplished in time past, great that they were, are all gone with time. If they did not change our character (remove the bad and add the good), then what value were they? It is today that we live, built on the foundation of all our yesterdays. If, today, we are not a better person than we were yesterday, yesterday's lessons were valueless. Then yesterday's choices we made were the wrong ones – undoubtedly moving us downhill rather than uphill towards heaven. Every choice has a consequence. We are either getting more like Jesus or more like satan. Each day contains God's challenge to grow more like Him. If we choose not to … answer that for yourself.

The Lord through His Spirit is so intimately involved inside us that He injects perfect guidance at every moment in time. This guidance is unique to each one of us. It is specific guidance for you as an individual, is not duplicated in any other human being, speaks your language perfectly, is specifically tuned to God's pre-planned route for you to take, is perfectly timed to deal with the negatives inside you and inject heavenly attitudes to build your divine nature (2 Peter 1:4), is designed for you, as you travel earth's surfaces, to fulfil good works which are exclusively yours, and brings increasing intimacy with your Lord and Saviour as you listen and do. There is no better way possible in the universe for any of us to travel than the one that the Holy Spirit is suggesting at this moment. If there is not one other human being who agrees with what the Lord is prompting inside you, don't listen to them. Go with Jesus.

Mind you, God has designed us to belong to each other, so, generally, you will find others who catch the vision the Lord has given us, so we will have companions along the way. But there will be times when they take a while to catch up with where the Lord is leading us.

In the same way that God specifically engineered conception, He specifically engineers our life on earth. How are we handling the troubles and difficulties that satan is throwing at us? If, perchance, our reactions to them are resentment, anger, bitterness, revenge, lust and such like, we are not yet fit for heaven. We have more to learn about God's kind of forgiveness and grace. Which means that we will have to continue living in satan's territory (he is the god of this world) until we have learned to select God's grace over satan's negatives.

Eileen and I have just lost a good friend. She died of cancer at far too young an age. So why did such a lovely Christian lady die? My perception is that she was far too good to remain on earth. We loved her ministry to us and wanted her to remain with us. But God has the long-term view. She had been altered by the Spirit and received His inputs so gladly that she was ready for heaven. I am not good enough yet and have more lessons to learn for me to go home right now. I still have more sharp edges to smooth off and some tasks to fulfil before I am qualified to leave this school of hard knocks called earth.

Please remember – God is Sovereign Lord of all, and His ways are perfect. Perfect in design, perfect in gentleness, perfect in humility, perfect in guiding, perfect in knowledge, perfect in understanding us through and through, perfect in His unique preparation of us for heaven, perfect in His love for us, and perfect in His support and control of all our surroundings. "And his ways are ways of gentleness, and all his paths are peace."

Jesus Christ is for each one of us. He has selected us from among the millions on earth, and He, our Bridegroom, is drawing us into His Kingdom and preparing wedding clothes for us. *"Let us rejoice and be glad and give him glory! For the wedding of the Lamb has come and his bride has made herself ready. Fine linen, bright and clean, was given her to wear. (Fine linen stands for the righteous acts of the saints)."* (Rev 19:7-8).

The one thing that I cannot yet fully understand is how God plans every human being so perfectly, yet loses so many. Their choices and their deeds do not follow His counsel or His ways, so His heaven would be hell for them. They will be excluded for ever from His Kingdom, and will never be part of the Bride of Christ. (Mind you, there is always time for them to repent. While they still have life, we can still have hope for them). It is a good thing that the

Lord has a perfect handle on all of their circumstances too. Because I haven't.

Isaiah says of the Lord *"A bruised reed he will not break and a smoking flax he will not quench."* (42:3). That is, God is the Great Encourager. We often see ourselves as of little value. There are so many humans around that I must be completely insignificant. But that is not the Lord's perspective. He knows that we are the peak of his creation. He has planned humans to belong in the Godhead with Him and to reign with Him over the new universe. We are of infinite value to Him – each one of us individually. Therefore He is not going to jeopardise our restoration by concentrating on unimportant things. You may have many things about you that annoy or frustrate me – habits, appearance, mannerisms, uncleanness, bad breath, irresponsibility etc - but they never frustrate the Lord. He deals so gently with the Now issue in our lives – the one thing at this moment that is necessary for us to grow in Him. Let me give you an example. I started biting my fingernails at the age of three. My Mum tried her best to rid me of it, and the habit must have annoyed many people throughout my years. I eventually gave it up in Perú when I was 46 years old. Before that it was not an important issue to the Lord. To have brought it up as an important issue before that could easily have quenched the tender smoking flax that represented my salvation.

God retains and honours our individual uniqueness. If we choose to have a messy home or a neat one, it does not worry Him half as much as it may worry other people. *"Why should my freedom be judged by another's conscience?"* (1 Cor 10:29). I can have a messy car or a messy desk, and if those are my choices, then that is fine with God. I recently stayed in a home of a married couple who were both doctors and who had two kids. They were very busy people. As a consequence, they had little time to keep their house spotless. It was clean but not tidy. I knew immediately that this was not an issue with the Lord; so it never became an issue with me. How could I possibly try to change what God is not trying to change?

What God is doing is enhancing and enriching our uniqueness.

You are amazing. You are special. You are wonderful. You are unique. Without you, to whom would I go for encouragement and love? I can barely wait for heaven to see the perfected you. Meanwhile, I love you just as you are. My acceptance of you is unconditional.

I learned that from Jesus..

God's Manifestation.

God made man. That demonstrates that God was infinitely bigger than man. So how was He going to show Himself to man, but still be recognised as God?

So, if you were God and had made all things and were in constant control of all things (yes, that big), how would you show yourself to one of your creatures – very much lesser than you were? I bet you wouldn't do it the way God did!

So how did He do it?

He became the nicest guy in the universe – without compromising any of His goodness.

He became a man. That was the first way He showed Himself to mankind. They could then *see* Him. And touch Him. And hear Him. And feel Him. Throughout His life, He showed Himself as being infinitely kind. He was empathetic, really concerned about everyone He met or who met Him. He was so helpful – He healed everyone who was sick or ill. *Every*one. He showed them how to become successful – that is, to do the same kinds of healings that He did, and use the same kind of system that He was so successful at. He was such delightful company. He was very unthreatening – to all those who were interested in Him. (Mind you, He seemed to be very threatening to many of those who disagreed with Him).

But to all who surrendered to His message, God through Jesus was very, very kind and endearing. All His ways were ways of gentleness and peace.

They still are.

Why? Why was there so little demonstration of enormous bigness? God wanted people to see Him *by Faith*. Not by sight. People in His day could see a very ordinary human being who showed no manifestations whatever of power, glory or anything enormous. They only saw His faith, and how effective that was. But in Himself, He was only ever kind, gentle, generous, and forgiving.

Anyone who wants to know God or know what He is like only need to turn to Jesus and see. The Jesus that appeared on earth two thousand years ago is the same Jesus who appears to you and me today. He is still gentle. He is still kind. He is still humble. He is still very helpful. He still brings His solutions very gently. What Jesus was and what He is to us today is the side of God that

He wants us to experience in our relationship with Him. God, as a man, is a very nice guy.

Now, if we read His Book and see what else God is, we will find that He is a God of power, majesty, inexpressible glory, frighteningly holy, and terrifyingly Sovereign over all things. We know that because He has told us that, and recorded the odd incident of that kind of thing in His book, the Bible. None of us have ever seen any of that. He occasionally gives us the odd bizarre miracle that shakes all our preconceptions by breaking through all our norms. But then God immediately springs back to His default position – kindness, gentleness, goodness and niceness. We wish, sometimes, that He would show us a little bit of His glory and power. (But then we would probably shrivel under its red-hot burning purity). But He insists that, so far as I can tell for all of our lives, He only wants to be known as nice. He hides all His power qualities from us. That, as I think of it, is also very kind of Him.

But it means that the God who has manifested Himself as Jesus wants the same kind of relationship with us that He wants us to have with each other. Kind. Appreciative. Ordinary. Normal. Nothing spectacular. Not in any way awesome. We can chat to Him as a buddy, and He does not mind at all. Indeed, He prefers that. That is the way He wants us to know Him. And He said, *"If you have seen me, you have seen my Father. I am just like Him and He is just like me."*

As the years zoom by in our relationship with Him, we become more and more amazed at His consistency. He is *always* nice. He is *always* kind. He *always* forgives, instantly, and without condemnation. In fact, the contrast with our own lives becomes more and more stark. He is *far* kinder that we ever are. He is *far* nicer than we have ever been. I get all goose-bumpy when I think that Jesus lived thirty plus years on earth and *never once sinned.* How desperately unlike me *that* is. The contrast between my character and His character shows itself more and more as my relationship deepens with Him. I am so unlike Him.

There are many Christians who think the approach I am recommending in this essay is very dishonouring to Jesus. They do not like a "pally" approach. But I am trying to be realistic. The Jesus I know and have known for many decades presents Himself as being very "normal". The only signs of His being enormous and terrifying consists in His being unchangeably good. He is permanently good, kind, gentle and "nice" forever. He is a friend who gently sees me through every difficulty without any rebukes, criticisms, condemnations or scoldings.

He hides His enormity and the "other" things He gets up to from me. I only know His companionship here on earth. God, through Jesus, is my *friend.*

But I want to be much more like Him. I have to stop being domineering. Stop being brutal. Be more gentle. Be more sympathetic. Be kinder. Honour others much more, and above myself. Promote everybody else. Be more helpful. Keep returning to Him in my silent, inner relationship with Him and feed off His grace, off His wholeness, off His healing. I just have to learn to forgive others, and, even more especially, forgive myself for all the stupid things I have done throughout my life. I want God to make me more and more like Jesus was and still is. If I can copy His lifestyle, I shall be OK, both here on earth and there in heaven. I want to be like God has shown Himself to be. The real Him inside loves me to bits. I want to love Him back in the same way. And I want to love my fellow travellers on earth just like He does too.

The gentle, kind and loving Jesus that I have known for many decades is also the great God of heaven and earth. So when I get to see Him, (which all of us will do the moment we die), He will not be any different from what He has always been to me. I will, of course, see His glory and His power then, but He will give me eyes that can see it without shrivelling up.

For those who love Jesus, God His Father only has a cuddle, a hug and a word of encouragement. If we have survived His challenging Kindergarten (our life on earth), and still remained faithful to Him despite all our failings and all the provocation, then we have won! Just survival and loyalty to Him will be good enough. He will be *very* pleased with us.

A Little glimpse of Jesus.

In the last chapter, I wrote that Jesus shows Himself as my Friend. We are "buddies" together. And that He has always shown Himself to mankind in that form, particularly when He was alive on earth, but now to us all. Despite what else He gets up to in His universe, His presentation of Himself to me, and to us, is very low key; He is down at our level. He is, as He said in Matt 11:29, *gentle and humble of heart.* I also said that there would be some who would object to my presentation of the King above all kings in that fashion. But I will not retract. The reality of the Jesus I have known for over sixty decades is my close and gentle *Friend.*

So, yesterday's Sunday morning Church service gave me another revelation, opening my toddler understanding to another perspective. God was not offended by my description of Jesus as my Buddy (it is impossible to offend God). But, very gently and very kindlily, He took me up to His heaven during the service.

The Lord took me into a huge hall with similar enormous rooms off it. I was like a little child going for the first time into a palace or cathedral, looking up, looking round, and stunned into complete silence because of the enormous size of the building, and feeling very, very small. There were no lights in the building. It was not dark, but it was like being in a house an hour after sunset, or an hour before dawn, what one of my Devon friends called dimpsy dark. The hall had no artifacts. It was plain and simple. But it was, simply, huge.

In addition, it was completely silent. It was awesomely silent. It was pregnant with silence. Not that there was about to be noise or music of any kind, or that there was any anticipation of anything else happening in it or to it – it was permanently quiet. And very still. It was as if I had to hold my breath to stand in there. The silence and calm filled the whole place.

It was not a cold silence, nor was it uncared for. It was warm and clean. It was not uninviting, but neither was it inviting. It just was, as if it had been there from the most ancient of times, even before eternity. It was full, but I had no idea what it was full of. It was complete in every aspect of its existence. Nothing could be added to it, and nothing could be taken away from it. The whole building and all the rooms were undecorated, but none of them needed to be. Everything about the whole place was complete in itself. It was simple and unsophisticated. It just was. It always had been.

Quiet. Silent. Calm. Enormous. Awesome. Breathtaking. Overwhelming. Full. Complete. Immoveable. Unchanging. Finished. Eternal.

"That," whispered God to me, "is a portrait of My Son Jesus. He is glad to be your friend, but He is never casual."

Tricky.

15

I am trying, at the moment, to write a novel about a man who went to heaven. My hero is in heaven and is about to create a new planet. That is where I have come unstuck immediately.

Can I create a planet without gravity? (There is no suggestion anywhere in my Bible that heaven contains gravity). If so, how do I keep my animals on it?

Do I want my hero to create animals at all? If so, do they reproduce? If so, how am I going to cope with over-population? So, if they can reproduce, I need to introduce time. Time means that things can be born, can live and can die to make room for more things that are born. But, in heaven, there is no time. So, how can I make a new creation that has no time? Or, if it has time, how do I introduce death?

On earth, death is a result of sin. It is punishment. So, do I introduce sin into my new planet, together with a suitable punishment? I notice that God dealt with sin right at the beginning of Adam's life, warning him that if he sinned, God would introduce death. So, the sin issue was finalised right at the start of our earth. That meant that death was part of the whole earth's system from the beginning. That tied in nicely with time, so that plants, animals and man could all die and be replaced by the next generations. So, how do I create, from my imagination, a planet without sin, without death, and without constant reproduction?

God got it all sorted from the beginning of this earth, and that is how and why it all works. I only know this system, because it is the only system that I have lived in all my life. I am having enormous difficulty to devise another brand-new system that either did not involve time, did not involve sin, did not involve death, probably did not involve gravity and did not involve reproduction. After all, heaven is without time, and, so far as I can tell from the scriptures, without reproduction. And certainly without death. Living beings in heaven, like angels, were all created individually. That is fine. But what do they do if they don't reproduce? Of course, they can invent stuff. But the only kind of inventiveness I know here on earth is one which is developed from previous inventions, and therefore involves time. So, how do I invent something which is perfect in the first place, never needs replacing, never grows old, and last for eternity? And would there have to be an end to inventions? My planet could get crammed full of stuff that never needed replacing.

So, what kind of creatures shall I invent? If they are lesser creatures (which all creatures have to be by definition), what would their purpose be? What magnificent talents should I give them? I could give them song. But the only kind of singing I know on this earth is one that uses time. That is, every song I know has a beginning, a middle and an end, and then they are done. Finished. That is a side-effect of time. How do I create songs or music that do not involve time?

And, on this earth I love children. (My love for them is not a sinful thing). I love their innocence, their purity of heart and therefore their cleanness of thinking. I love and admire their directness, their inability to hide what is going on inside them, and so on. Jesus Himself loved little children, and wanted to cuddle them in His arms. Indeed, He told us sophisticated adults to grow down and become like little children (Matt 18 refers). Be innocent. Do not clutter your lives with uglinesses. Then, on this earth, children grow up. They lose their innocence and therefore their beauty. In most cases, that is such a sadness. So, on my new eternal planet, I have decided that my children will never grow up. They will be cuddly and cute for ever.

I notice that sci-fi writers have got gravity in all their new civilisations. No one, not even in a star ship, has weightlessness. They all stick to the floor or the land. And they all have time. They are all based on this creation's parameters and limitations. But if, as a Christian, I am going to live in heaven, without apparent gravity, without apparent time and without any death, how do I devise a creation that is more like heaven than earth without the only tools that I have in my hands and that mirror this earth's tools exactly?

Then what about vegetation? Earth's ecosystem really is a complete ecosystem. Everything is interrelated. Plants grow, insects and birds help to scatter the seeds, fungi spring up inside the ground that, living or dying, feed other plants or insects or animals, and the whole is governed by rain, by sunshine, by seasons, by water, by air by itself interlaced with all of itself, and it all *works*. Earth's ecosystem is one whole system, everything interrelated to everything else. This earth truly is unbelievably amazing in the way that it all holds together. And the air continues to stick to the earth, is continually being replenished and cleaned by the vegetation, seeds germinate season after season to feed the whole population of animals, birds, insects, man, and even itself in never-ending circles of recovery. It is astonishing that, all my life this earth has fed me, watered me, kept me alive by air, found work for me and tools to work with, and has never lost any of it. So how can I invent another planet that doesn't do the same? One that is different from the only things that I know?

And then I have mathematics. Mathematics on this earth is complete. That is, everything that has been made, from the galaxies in the sky to the insects in the forests to the single atom, are all held together by a chain and system of mathematics that cannot be broken, and that can be used. Nothing holds together without laws — mathematical laws. We found that the mathematics of earth worked well in space when we went to the moon. And we presume that they also work on Andromeda in space as well. It is *one* system. And it is also eternal. That is, all mathematic laws have been putting things together and holding things together from the beginning of creation, and will last to the end of creation, because it is one system. When earth dies, its mathematics will also die. So, if I am going to create a planet in heaven without gravity, without time and without death, I am also going to have to invent a brand-new mathematics that is consistent with all of that, and holds all things in heaven together in the same way that earthen mathematics holds all earthen things together. The reality is that there must be a mathematics of the Spirit that differs from earthen mathematics, and that none of us knows anything about it at all.

All I can do is to copy the sci-fi parameters and use features that I already know without comment, and merely change the creatures and the way they look and what their tasks might be. I do not have the imagination nor the ability to *invent* a system that does not include earth's basic features. Unless, of course, I get revelation from God Himself. He, of course, can invent anything, and make it work. I can't. Anyway, my Bible tells me this: *"However, as it is written: 'What no eye has seen, what no ear has heard, and what no human mind has conceived' — the things God has prepared for those who love him — these are the things God has revealed to us by his Spirit."* In other words, God has not told us, and has no intention of telling us, what is going to happen in heaven, and what He has in mind to invent — unless He chooses to reveal a tiny bit of it to me, trying to write a novel about heaven.

I'm sure you can see my difficulty. I now need revelation direct from heaven. Just what am I going to put into my novel to make it as near as I can to the real heaven?

You now need to read my three novels to see what the Lord came up with.

Building.

Let us think about houses or other buildings for a moment.

They need planning permission. Then they need an architect/designer. Then they need a building contract with a builder. Then the building firm starts to construct the edifice, and takes time and care in its construction, especially with the foundations, until it is finished. Not until then is it ready for use. During its period of use it will need maintaining, because, on this earth, entropy insists that everything tends to decay to chaos unless energy is applied to prevent it. Eventually the building will be taken down after a few decades, demolished, and something else will replace it. All of the life of the building covers a predictable period of time.

An individual human being is described in scripture as God's building (1 Cor 3:9). I want to follow through some of the similarities between what we do with a building on earth and what God does with a human being for heaven.

First, we need planning permission. Let me be blunt here – God chooses those who will eventually live with Him in heaven. Actually, God *has chosen*. We have been chosen *"…in him (Jesus Christ) before the creation of the world…"* (Eph 1:4). That doctrine, as it stands, is very often very offensive to many human beings. But we have to include all the other Biblical additions that are involved in that statement, and it cannot stand alone. We also have choice; and that is included in God's choice. When our choice marries God's choice, permission for heaven is granted – exactly the same as when our choice of building matches the County Council's permission. Also, from other scriptures, I never read that God deliberately chooses any human being to go to hell; all go to hell by their own choice. Responding to God's call on a life invariably involves repentance, and few of us like repenting. God, who sees things from the end as well as from the beginning, knows those who will not repent, will not have Jesus reign over them, and prefer their own destiny over God's destiny for them. For them, all earth becomes an extension of hell – mainly because God's reconciliatory goodness is never involved in their lives. The good and forgiveness people refuse to receive from God on earth they will also refuse after death when stark reality confronts them with clarity. God cannot ever reach those kinds of people with His love and reconciliation.

God, who knows the end from the beginning, chooses those who choose Him in their lives. For sentient people like us, we only get God's eternal planning permission in our lives for heaven if we also desire it.

Secondly, every building needs designing. (Isn't that so obvious?) That is why God has designed every human being who has ever lived on earth. Every human being is unique – there are no two of us alike. It is not just our bodies that are designed (and we all look and act differently) – it is our souls too. What our talents and abilities are, and what our desires are are unique to each of us and confined inside this moving tent called "body". Because God is personally in charge of every human conception (*that* sperm for *that* egg at *that* moment in time), I believe that every single human being on earth has the ability and the capacity, and will have the opportunity to meet God on earth. And, if they are willing, they have the ability to surrender to His sovereign love. Because God is fair, He gives everyone the opportunity. But He does not control their response. Everyone chooses their own hell or their own heaven. That is, with God or away from Him. To love Him more than themselves, or to love themselves more than Him. The building must be useful to the Designer, or, eventually, it will be torn down and binned.

The **third** thing that a building needs is a contract between the architect and a builder. For a human life, that contract is made between God and parents. God chooses *those* parents to bring up *those* children better than anyone else can. Because those parents have generated that child, they are the best at bringing him or her up. All that organisation was designed by God from the beginning. (We really mess up our responsibilities when children are brought up without a father or a mother, or when homosexuals bring up children). Every child needs a father and a mother, and the same father and the same mother that conceived them. Biologically it is impossible to generate a human child without a father's sperm and a mother's egg. It is also impossible to bring up a child as God would wish without those same two doing the bringing up. Parents have a contract with God to take their own child(ren) into adult maturity with a knowledge of the God who designed all of them, and a lifestyle that adds to society, and does not detract from it.

Fourth, the whole building needs all the rules and regulations incorporated into it. The foundations are critical for the life of the building, and must obey all the mathematical rules for buildings. All the drains and facilities must go in before anything is built on top of the foundations. So it is with children. Parents are responsible for knowing what is the right way to live on planet earth. God has made mathematical rules that govern architects, and moral rules that govern human beings. They are absolutes. Mathematic rules are absolute – to disobey them or ignore them will eventually collapse the building. So with moral and Biblical rules. To live an unrighteous life, either in the parents or in their children, will end them in hell eternally. Don't mess with the rules! Don't mess with the Word of God!

Fifth, preparation and construction takes time before the building is ready for use. It came to me early this morning that our Primary School age is the age of instruction. We are under our parents' authority, and, in a good sense, we belong to them. They teach us and form our characters. Our secondary school age is when our parents have to start letting us go because our adult characters will then be developing into what God wants us to do in life. Very few of us do what our parents did. Most of us choose careers that, often, mystify our parents. Graduating to University or college takes us into the completion of our training for adulthood, and we then leave the nest for good and travel to the ends of the earth doing what God wants us to do, or what our talents enable us to do, despite our parent's wishes or knowledge.

Jesus is our illustration. He was obedient to his parents until he was twelve. He then did His Bar-Mitzvah in Jerusalem with the Elders. That is the Jewish transition into adulthood. He then learned carpentry with God and step-father Joseph, and then took over both the business and the family (as the oldest son) when Joseph died. All that was preparation for His adult ministry. At about the age of thirty, God called Him into His full-time ministry, which was alien to Mary and His brothers and sisters (see Mark 3:21). Not only was Jesus perfect, the pattern for His life was the perfect blueprint for every life on earth.

Sixth, we have a full-time calling and ministry. Or, for those who do not know Jesus, a job. The channelling of our job is dependent on our giftings. We work all through our lives on earth, even when we have officially retired. Work never ends. This is when the building that has been built becomes useable and useful. In Jesus' life that only took three years. For a Christian, access to the treasures of heaven need to come in daily (your house needs regular maintenance). "Live by the Spirit" says our Bibles (Gal 5:16). That is the only way to keep our eternal fire refuelled, stoked up and burning bright.

Finally, we die. The building gets knocked down and a new one takes its place.

Actually we all live in death on this earth. Everything we did yesterday has gone and is already dead. Our contribution to life on earth, and to the life of earth, is fleeting. Our ambition in our youth, when we teem with initiative and energy, was to change the world for the better, and we thought we could do it. But nobody can. Even Presidents get voted out or die, and they are always replaced by another.

To me the lesson is crystal clear: this earth is never the place in which we can leave a mark, however good our preparation and however talented we are. I was looking at a statue of a Boer-war general the other day. He was a great man in his day. But now? He at least has a statue (which I will never have). But there is no memory of him left. He is dead to earth and earth is dead to him. If he did not place his trust in the eternal God, he has no eternal significance either.

Nor will you or I have, if we do not secure our life's unique treasures in God's eternal bank.

Disarming.

Colossians 2:15 says: *"And having disarmed the powers and authorities, he made a public spectacle of them, triumphing over them by the cross."*

How did the Cross of Jesus do that?

To disarm is to take away weapons. So what weapons do the demonic powers and authorities possess – presumably in their warfare against mankind?

Clearly, the key one is sin. Any human being who sins comes into the death of separation from God, because they leave Him out of all those decisions. Then they have to live out the eternal consequences for each one they do. So demon spirits who have tempted an individual to sin, and had success, have gained another recruit for the hell that they live in, which both will inherit in its fullness. (Logically, I cannot see why they relish doing that. They are themselves in eternal separation from God. But why do they wish that all mankind should join them? Isn't their separation dark enough for them, to desire to perpetuate their hatred more)?

Hatred is one of the consequences of their separation from all that is good, and good can only be from the God of all goodness. It is that separation that is the key to all sin. Inside God's love and heart is only unity, love, contentment, happiness, fulfilment, and all things wonderful. Outside His love and heart there is only awfulness of every description. It is the separation that is the key.

Demon spirits are successful in their temptation because mankind, all of us, are weak. We are also ignorant of their presence, and ignorant of the nature of temptation. Sin is eternally terminal. They know that. We don't. We are blind to most things eternal.

So how did the cross of Jesus deal with those things?

1. Jesus took on separation from God by the command of God, thus experiencing legitimately all the separation that is sin in mankind.

2. Jesus was able to do that, in principle, for all of mankind because He was the perfect representative of Adam's race before God.

3. Jesus consequently took the punishment that all sin in Adam's race deserve, and went to hell for three days. Therefore all accusation from satan towards mankind is annulled. The price has been fully paid. There can be no condemnation for any sin for all those in Jesus Christ.

4. Jesus can now forgive *every* sin in every human being who turns to Him for forgiveness. (But only for those who turn to Jesus for forgiveness). All demonic weaponry has been removed. No accusation is valid any longer. Satan has been silenced for ever.

So this is the way I see it: the Cross of Jesus dealt with all sin in an individual, dealt with all death in that individual and also dealt with Law, which highlighted their sin and death. So, for that individual, repentance and rebirth have erased every cause of separation from God. God and that person are now One. God has caused them to take on the unity of the Trinity. For him/her, Law, sin and death are now totally irrelevant. All work is from God and for God. Satan has nothing to accuse them of.

So then, how did the cross make a public spectacle of the satanic actions?

When the full truth of the rationale behind Jesus' righteous death became fully known, the wickedness of the demonic authorities in the heavenly places became fully exposed, along with the filth and the venom of High Priest Caiaphas and the Jewish Sanhedrin. What they had at that moment was the triumph of evil, exposed in broad daylight for all to see. What that moment became was the darkest wickedness that there has ever been. No twisted historical reporting can ever change that. Even if people know nothing of the incident, they all know that what satan and his followers did was evil, wicked and, simply, wrong. It was a public spectacle of iniquity and malice. *"None of the rulers of this age understood it, for if they had, they would not have crucified the Lord of glory."* (1 Cor 2:8).

Finally, then, how did the cross triumph over the demonic forces?

The greatest triumph that satan and his demonic forces had over mankind was to tempt Eve successfully in the Garden of Eden. Adam felt he had to align himself to her by eating the forbidden fruit, and so, in his mind and heart, rescue her. (Remember, Eve had been part of Adam in the beginning, so he was trying to rescue himself). But he rescued her into hell. Adam's sin released satan to perpetuate his evil throughout mankind and throughout the earth forever. Sin became rampant, and resulted in the extermination of all mankind except eight in The Flood. Sin was then restricted from proliferating too much and too fast after The Flood by God introducing Law into mankind. Man's conscience became the controlling factor, and no one likes feeling guilty. Sin remained, but it was reduced and curtailed. Satan still had his victories throughout earth.

But now the cross of Jesus dealt fully with sin, with Law and with death. It neutralised all three and removed them for all those who surrender their lives to Jesus. Sin, Law and Death remain for all those still living in separation from God. But for all those who have Jesus living in their hearts as Lord, all sin is forgiven, Law no longer applies, death has been removed, they have been reborn from above by God, the Holy Spirit has been injected into them eternally, they have come under God's personal covering, they are forgiven for any further sin, their limitations are ignored, and they fully inherit every promise that God has made. God calls that "salvation" or "rescue". *"For as in Adam all die, so in Christ all will be made alive."* (1 Cor 15:22).

"So will it be with the resurrection of the dead. The body that is sown is perishable, it is raised imperishable; it is sown in dishonour, it is raised in glory; it is sown in weakness, it is raised in power; it is sown a natural body, it is raised a spiritual body." (1 Cor 15:42-44). The Cross and Resurrection of Jesus Christ destroyed the whole fabric of satan's many millennia of wickednesses, and introduced a new humanity in Jesus that was forgiven and then separated from wickedness and united to God. *"Therefore, if anyone is in Christ, he is a new creation. The old has passed away; behold, the new has come."* (1 Cor 5:17). Satan is disarmed for ever.

Gifts.

It came to me from the Lord that I should look at some of the gifts that He gave so that all of us can live comfortably throughout our lives.

Earth. All of earth has been given. None of it is of man's making. It is man's celestial home.

Gravity. Isn't it good that everything sticks downwards? Ever thought what it would be like if it didn't?

Sun. Isn't it so good to have heat? The distance of the sun from the earth is just right. 1% further away and we would freeze; 1% closer and we would boil. And there are all sorts of things coming out of the sun that we are shielded from: cosmic radiation, gamma radiation, solar flares, gravitation, and so on. So what arrives on earth does the earth good. It's a wonderful gift!

Water. Every living thing on earth needs water to continue to live. It was the first chemical that God created on earth. Its abundance governs all life on earth. It has astonishing properties.

Chemistry. We can manipulate material on earth, without which we would have no shelter, no transport, no things. All material has been given.

Mathematics. This whole universe is governed by mathematical laws, many of which we have been able to unravel and then use. Without mathematics, there would be no continuity in anything. All physics laws are mathematically based. Man has discovered mathematics, but not created it. If it hadn't been there from the beginning, nothing would have survived.

Bodies. None of us chose to live. (We can, of course, choose to die. But that would be silly). None of us chose the shape, gender, or details of any of our bodies. They were given. We use them, misuse them and take them for granted. We think they are ours. But they are not – they are gifts. And only temporary ones too!

Sleep. How lovely is sleep! It refreshes tired bodies. It forgets troubles. It passes time. It also slows down much evil in the world of darkness. Mother Teresa survived on four hours of sleep a night. When asked how she did it, she replied, "I sleep fast."

Talents. None of us chose our talents or our limitations. They were given.

We can, of course, choose not to use them, or we can choose to misuse them. Everyone has some.

Air. The way that we continue to live by breathing is remarkable. And the fact that there is enough air still on earth, and that hasn't drifted away into space, is a gift we cannot live without. Nor can any other living creature or plant on earth. The biological apparatus inside our bodies that uses air is remarkable; oxygen keeps our bodies clean and, through the carbon dioxide we breathe out, gets rid of pollutants from inside our bodies. We are all internal combustion engines. Also, without air, we cannot speak to one another.

Vegetation. Trees replenish the oxygen in the atmosphere. Most greenery provides food for both humans and animals. Isn't it wonderful that green things keep living things living?

Insects. Some insects are annoying. But all of them, in their own way, form a huge empire of tiny living things that process vegetation and stop decay in dying flora. Bees and other insects of that kind, of course, fertilise plants. In fact, the whole environment has nothing to do with man's initiative. The produce of earth cannot be sustained without insects.

Seasons. Without the seasons there would be no harvest and no food.

Day/Night. This is governed by the rotation of the earth and the tilt of the earth's axis in relation to the sun. A day that is longer would fry us all. A night that is longer would freeze us all. The margins are tiny. There is absolutely nothing we can do to alter the rotation of the earth.

Beauty. Everything that God makes is beautiful. Every nation on earth has its own beauty, none of which is duplicated anywhere else on earth. No mountain ranges are similar. No views are similar. Many things that man has made are also beautiful, and the variety staggers us. Beauty is a gift. God gave it to us as an added extra.

Animals. Domestic animals enhance our lives, and most of us love them. But God has also given us wild animals. For what purpose? Why is a giraffe? But they all make for a colourful and creative environment in which man can live, and give us all a responsibility to care for their survival.

Forgiveness. There is not one perfect human being on earth, or ever has been. Only Jesus. That is why only He can offer forgiveness for our indiscretions, our failures and even our wickednesses. He made this earth. He made us as humans. He died that we might be forgiven. And He forgives us – if only we would let Him.

If you think about it, there is practically nothing that affects our lives and enables us to live that is man initiated. There are, of course, cars and aeroplanes. But the material that we make them with is all given. Everything is already given. Of course, we plant and harvest. But the ability of plants to reproduce is a gift that comes from God. And, if I read Genesis correctly, all of it was established before Adam was created. He moved into a fully prepared and completed environment. He had the right number of arms and legs, was given the ability to walk bipedally (on two legs), his children could learn a language within two years of being born, could breathe automatically, could process food, and could devise things through thought and manipulation. Mankind arrived fully equipped. All was gifted. What a thoughtful, careful, and creative God we have – if we want Him.

We were also given the ability to be thankful. That is a gift that is far too often ignored throughout mankind.

Goodness.

*"**T**he good is uncreated; it never could have been otherwise; it has no shadow of contingency; it lies, as Plato said, on the other side of existence. It is the **Rita** of the Hindus by which the gods themselves are divine, the **Tao** of the Chinese from which all realities proceed. But we, favoured beyond the wisest pagans, know what lies beyond existence, what admits no contingency, what lends divinity to all else, what is the ground of all existence, is not simply a law but also a begetting love, a love begotten, and the love which, being between these two, is also imminent in all those who are caught up to share the unity of their self-cause life. God is not merely good, but goodness; goodness is not merely divine, but God." C.S. Lewis, "**Christian Reflections**".*

I hope you got all that. It would pay us all to read it again and again until we understand it thoroughly, and until it has become a part of our souls.

Goodness was never created. It permeates the whole of creation. Love, I guess, is the foundational root of creation; that is, God created because He loved. But everything that was created, from the basic elements of matter (neutrons, protons, electrons etc) to the fiercest nuclear explosions that make up stars, every thing is good.

It is not possible for it to be otherwise. It is impossible to find or even conceive of anything in the whole creation that is in any way bad, or ugly, or incidental, or irrelevant. All is complete, integrated, belonging – all is part of everything else, and all is part of the whole. There is nothing missing in the whole of creation. Everything in creation has a purpose, a *raison d'être*, and without it – even the tiniest detail - the whole would not function. Or it would function like a bird with a broken wing.

I like the quote from Plato above: goodness belongs on the other side of creation. Nothing can exist without goodness, any more than concrete can exist without cement, or a tree can exist without water. Or water can exist without oxygen. Or … there are countless other examples that you can recall. Goodness permeates everything. Indeed, without goodness there would be no creation.

That is because God is good. Or, better, God is goodness. Everything that exists reflects the character of the God who made it. So, everything will also include love, patience, grace, kindness, compassion, forgiveness, reconciliation, integration. Goodness permeates all those. And all those permeate goodness. When the Bible says that God is One, that is part of what it means.

But here the word reconciliation implies evil – that people have gone astray and need to be reconciled. So what part does evil play in goodness? I think, first of all, that evil cannot ever alter or replace goodness. To destroy the goodness that lies beneath and behind creation would be to destroy creation itself. Therefore its goodness is unapproachable. All evil can do is to twist goodness, misuse it, misappropriate it, bend it. So, a tsunami is a misappropriation of good water. According to Job 1:13-19, satan can twist goodness for his own evil purposes. But he can never destroy it.

And what about us? Well now, I find it strange but true that everyone wants to be or do good. There is an instinct locked inside every human being that to be good is better than to be bad. In a contorted kind of way, even those whole life philosophies include killing people, think that they are doing good by killing. Religious people of varying kinds, persuasions and intensities (other than Christians) kill many other people (especially Christians) for a reason and a logic that escapes me; but they consider those deeds (which I consider to be evil) are the good and right thing to do. Do you see how goodness can never be destroyed, but it can be twisted? Satan is good at it. (And there, you see, I have used the word "good" to demonstrate evil; satan is good at evil).

C.S. Lewis says that Goodness is God and God is goodness. Goodness is unavoidable. So, taking the philosophy that some things are better joining if they are unavoidable, would it not be the best thing in the world for everyone to integrate themselves with the God who created, the God who loved, the God who cares, the God whose essence is goodness?

To be good means we have to seek after goodness. To love is to surrender to the lover. To be the best is to be fully, gladly, delightedly empty of oneself and filled with all the fullness of the God who is altogether goodness. That is, as I see it, the only way to understand our whole rationale for existence, and the only way to understand creation.

And, consequently, choosing to belong to the Goodness who is inside this good creation, is to fully Be.

The Key to Everything.

Thе title reminds me of a phrase that very erudite and clever scientists have expressed: they are researching for, working on and hunting for "The Theory of Everything." So let me solve that concept straight away, but from God's perspective.

In His Heaven before He created time and space, God was a three-some. They lived in love together. They then decided that their love needed to extend. It was not enough to be alone together, although they never experienced loneliness. It just meant that Their love longed for others to love. And because there were no others, They decided to create them.

First They created beings that had the same life system as Themselves - all the angelic throng. All were spiritual, because God is spirit (John 4:24). There was no such thing as Time in those days. God had in mind a single plan in which He could give and receive love from created beings. That plan has never changed, simply because God is still outside of Time; He sees the end from the beginning (although, with Him, there is no such thing as an end or a beginning; He is "I AM").

Then He (They) decided to make a physical creation, different from the spirit beings and the spiritual environment that He had already made. God thought through very carefully what kind of creatures He would want in His physical creation, and what sort of environment He would want them to live in. They would need to belong together as one unit, even though they would be of different kinds and species. Then He needed someone to rule over the physical creation, to develop and run it according to His own abilities and wisdom. That ruler would need to be of a kind and form that He Himself could inhabit, should that ever become necessary. And the whole would be a relationship of love and respect, in which they and He would operate together. His plan was that He should remain pro-actively involved in the development of His creation, but delegate work appropriately to the creatures. That leader would love and serve the creation on God's behalf.

So God made the earth and the universe, after which He made man.

God put man in a limited location (like a planet he could not easily escape from), with limited resources to start with, and gave him rulership over the whole planet. So the creation needed to be vast enough to test man's abilities and capacities. Man was small enough to do a job of work responsibly, but big enough to be able to do it. So, because God was God, He created a perfect creation, perfect in the microscopic and perfect all the way through to the cosmic. He also made man perfect, with enormous ability and extensive capacity, and with love.

It was a temporary creation, a kind of school in which God could test His creatures, and see if they would love Him back. In addition, God would place His spiritual beings – angels - as overall spiritual supervisors. They were fully conversant with Him, lived in His presence in the spiritual realm, and would operate as messengers and helpers to all the physical creatures that He had made.

Because the nature of God's kind of love is voluntary, His creatures, especially mankind, needed to know alternatives. For example, what if man chose not to love God back? Choice had to be fair and real.

So what was going to be the relationship that God wanted for man in man's control of God's earth? God had made the earth and all the other creatures in it, bracketed the whole lot in Time so that everything would continually change, and God wanted man to be His eyes, ears, lips, hands and feet on His physical earth to sort it out, control it, love it, develop and organise it for Him consistently. Where God was perfectly capable of sorting everything out for Himself, He chose to have others – angels and man – to do it for Him. Then love would be both ways. But because His was the creation, the only way that the creation could develop perfectly was that both men and angels would listen to God's instructions and solve the ever-changing problems of Time His way. Everything would then work perfectly.

There was one last thing to be completed. God's kind of love needed to be voluntary, as I have pointed out. So both men and angels had to be given choice. Where there is no alternative, there is no choice.

It so happened that the greatest created being so far, the fearsome Cherub named Lucifer, was placed in charge of the earth, because God saw that the central and most important part of His creation (earth) needed the best help it, and man, could get. There is an ancient Pharisaic tradition (which is not found in the Bible) that Lucifer objected to God's putting such a high priority on man, especially above all the spirit beings, that he decided to try to take over the creation himself. In his view, God's system was unjust and incorrect. He had choice, and chose independence from God and to be independent of God. He then immediately became eternally dark. He did not lose his job of overseeing earth and mankind, and is still with us today. But it is impossible for him to be good, as God defines good, in any way. (Biblically, see Isaiah 14:11-15).

God's method of supervision by the angels to man lay in the restriction that the supervisors could never control the physical realm without permission. That is, no spirit being, including Lucifer, could ever command mankind what to do. Areas of influence were very strictly boundaried, and angels had no permission to encroach on man's territory. The angels could only make suggestions. That ensured that every creature, physical and spiritual, would be personally responsible for their own destinies. That limitation God adhered to Himself. That meant that man, having the same choice that all the angels had, was personally responsible for responding in love to the God who had given him existence. Only in that way could God's kind of love be adequately reflected in His creatures.

It is uncertain whether God planned that this present creation would be the final one. The incorporation of Time in its construction meant that matters and issues passed by every second, extending the choice of love and obedience to one a second over many years of a human life-time. Therefore a life-time would be filled with choices to love and serve God every second. Earth was a testing ground of love for created man.

Unfortunately, man proved to be as fickle as Lucifer. Now that Lucifer had decided to go his own way, rather than God's way, his suggestions to man became suggestions of independence from God, rather than love for God. Lucifer was renamed satan, the accuser, or the devil. Satan can only tempt after the manner of his own evil. There is no other kind of evil. The choice for all is simple – to love and serve God or to live independently of, and rebellion towards God.

The choice of Adam and Eve to discard God's instructions and eat the forbidden fruit in their initial home in the Garden of Eden, was a tragedy of immense magnitude. The consequence was death. That consequence still applies. Adam's choice was fully independent; that is, uninfluenced by anyone else. As was Lucifer's. But it brought death to all of Adam's descendants, to the environment of earth, and eventually, to the whole cosmos.

But God was prepared for this eventuality.

God had made the creation in love and for love. He had made man and the angels perfectly, also in love and for love. So, instead of erasing both the creation and the creatures, His love determined to continue with His original plan. That required the *sacrifice* of love.

But how could rebellion be neutralised? By love. If it could be done, man could again choose to love and serve God rather than retain his independence and reject Him. Man could still choose backwards, reversing his inherited rebellion. In an environment of complete goodness, choice had to include the alternative of evil; now, in an environment of complete evil, choice had to include the alternative of goodness. But God's perfect justice also needed to be satisfied, and there was no one in the whole creation who could be good enough to do that. Only Himself. All of God's creatures were too limited. The depth of love and determination that was required was only possible by God Himself. So God Himself paid the price of love. Jesus, one of the Trinity, humbled Himself, downsized, became a man, entered time (at exactly the right moment), and volunteered to die on a Roman Cross.

That Cross was the perfect neutralisation of all evil. It paid for and removed every barrier to fulfilling God's original vision, and opened the door for mankind to return to God's planned design and serve God on His earth in a love bond. Please note that there was no redemption for satan or any of his dark angels. Only man. Jesus became a *man*.

But man had to access that redemption. When once an individual becomes aware that there is a possibility of heaven for him/her, all that is left is choice. People have to *choose* heaven instead of hell. That is, choose for God to direct them in love, rather than choosing to continue to direct their own ways. That choice is not possible without God first revealing Himself to individuals.

Through that redemption, God's original vision could be fulfilled for man. But not using the original creation. That was too dead to be redeemed. So God planned a new creation in which mankind could still serve Him in love. God's love ensured that the new man would be quite unlike the original man. No longer living in poverty, destitution and darkness, in the miniscule incapability of his personal brain, the new man would be remade into princes, princesses, God-like creatures, reborn with the very nature of God Himself. They would *"know even as they are fully known."* (1 Cor 13). They would be His family. No longer three; now countless numbers. But all physical as well as spiritual, along with their Lord, Jesus; all royalty; all glorious; all magnificent; all perfect in mind and body; all transformed, both in body and soul, by love. God's love and ability would never be thwarted and never be changed. The whole of this creation is now set up to find human beings whom God could love and who would gladly serve Him back in love. There is no other purpose in living. What God asks us to *do* while alive on earth is secondary and almost irrelevant. All work is individual anyway, unique and uncopiable.

Graduation day at death is, simply, pass or fail. The single issue is crystal clear, and very simple (on the same level as the prohibition in the Garden of Eden not to eat the fruit of that one tree). Has an individual chosen God's redemption or not?

The key to everything? The unchanging, unalterable and undiminished love and will of God.

Epilogue.

Mathematics is a phenomenal thing. Mathematics governs everything in the universe. It is the one stable issue undergirding all laws, physics, chemistry and all the other sciences. Like "sums" in Primary School, the result is either right or wrong, and there is no middle ground. A correct mathematical undergirding of every created thing makes that undergirding inerrantly true. It is also either right or wrong, and cannot be quibbled with. Any issue in creation that does not have that mathematic confirmation is probably error.

Some issues, mind you, struggle to find any mathematics involved. Creation disciplines like psychology may have trouble locating and analysing the mathematics undergirding them. But the physical areas involved in psychology – neurons and the nervous system, for example – hang together mathematically in the human body. The whole of creation is made solid, reliable, predictable, analysable, and certain by the mathematics behind them, whether those mathematics have yet been discovered or analysed by man or not. The formulae have existed from the first day of creation. It is the mathematics that has ensured that the creation actually works and has actually continued working throughout time. Mathematics undergirds everything. So when a person catches a ball, or a car driver avoids a collision, the mathematical formulae racing through their minds, enabling them to function correctly, are huge, complex and, often, unwritten. The brain works it out without the analysis into formulae. A good thing too in the microseconds that are involved.

Without mathematics, nothing holds together. An evolutionist is going to struggle to determine where mathematical laws originated. "It just does" is not good enough. There must have been an intelligence behind the formulae, first to create them, then to involve them in everything made, then to ensure that the mathematics are superior to the things made, and lastly to enable mankind, over the centuries, to discover them, analyse them and write them down for the rest of us. That intelligence created Life, basing Life's continued existence and function on unchanging constants that overarch, undergird, and oversee everything. Mathematics reigns over all physical existence.

Of course, I cannot find anywhere in my Bible that says that God is a mathematician. But it is obvious that it is He, the Creator, who also has ensured that His creation continues to exist by providing the stabilising phenomenon called mathematics. God is the supreme Mathematician. And, if we individually wish to travel down the road of analysing the mathematics, or even the road of a deeper relationship with God Himself, we can find full human contentment in both. Both will lead to Him like searchlights focus on an aircraft at night.

Anyone can find that personal relationship with God through the marvels of science. The world we live in is truly amazing in every discipline man has so far analysed. And still no one knows exactly what Life is. We have it. We use it. We enjoy it. We are alive. So is God, if only we would find Him. Nothing "just happened" in this beautiful and brilliant universe we inhabit.

Mathematics, like Law, is a "thing". It has no personality. Although it is phenomenal, God is more phenomenal, and much nicer, than mathematics. God is love, as well as clever. He longs to get to know each one of us, and mathematics is a very good place to start that journey. Being intelligent or clever is never good enough. God, the supreme intelligence, is also personal. A personal relationship with Him is not dependent on our abilities, but on our surrender to His love and forgiveness.

That is not just my song; it is the song and dance of the whole universe.

About the author.

133

Dick Bell was born in Kenya of a British family. His major love was aeroplanes, and, after his secondary schooling at Rossall in the UK, joined the RAF as a pilot. He became a Christian as a cadet at the RAF College Cranwell. He left the RAF after 20 years and became the main Bible Teacher at a Christian Conference Centre in Devon called Upcott, where he taught mainly children and teenagers for 26 years. He is married with one daughter and two grandsons. During his time at Upcott he took part in four Hovercraft expeditions on appropriate rivers across the world, under the leadership of Mike Cole OBE. Following the last expedition to Nicaragua, in 2000 he was called by God to take up full-time Missionary work there, where he founded the UK charity SIFT. His Missionary remit was four-fold – Initiate, Develop, Establish, Delegate. That enabled him to hand over the charity and begin a final new agricultural work on the Island of Ometepe in Nicaragua, where he also founded a new Church. He was prompted to write all the chapters in the Two-trees Series of books by the Holy Spirit since becoming a commuting Christian Missionary. He was granted an MBE in 2014 for his work in the Third World.

www.ingramcontent.com/pod-product-compliance
Lightning Source LLC
Chambersburg PA
CBHW061303120726

48001CB00001B/450